Model Railroad Layouts for N, HO, O & G Scale

Fourth Edition

72
73
81

By: Mike Kraft

There are lots of various ways you can design your layout based on the amount of space you have available or the type of operating you wish to do so we have tried to cover some of the most popular with the track plans in this book. Be sure to also checkout our bonus resources section at the end of the book for other great resources and exclusive discounts from the best brands in the business. This fourth edition includes track plans in N, HO, O & G scale along with layout dimension and the necessary parts list for the brand and track type utilized for nearly all plans to further assist in building your layout.

1. N SCALE ATLAS TR2 TRACK 45" X 69"

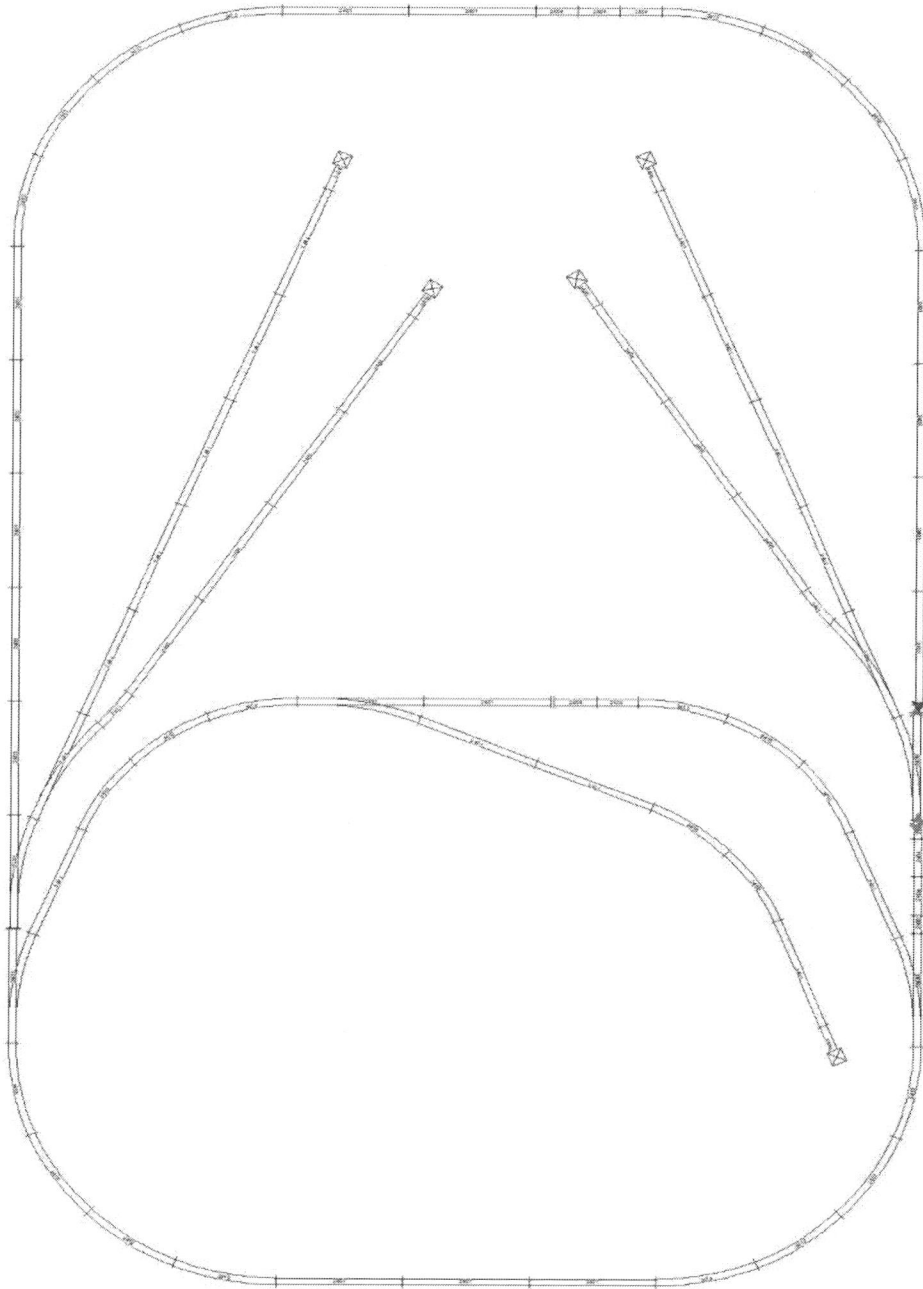

2. N SCALE ATLAS TR2 TRACK 58" X 56"

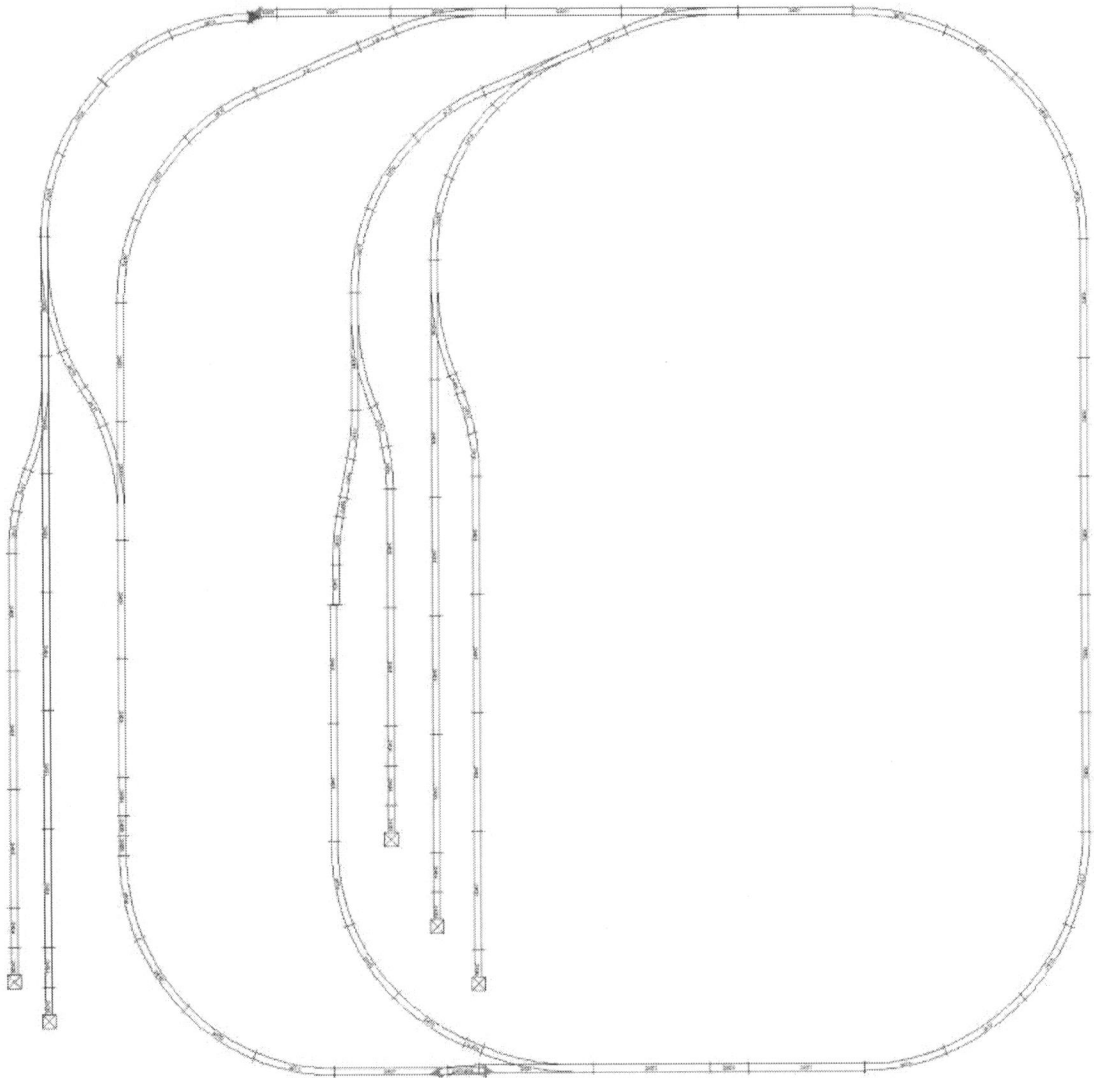

3. N SCALE ATLAS TR2 TRACK 68" X 17"

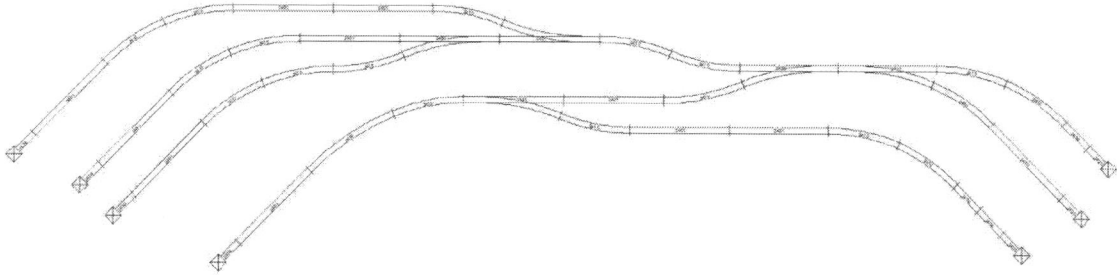

4. N SCALE ATLAS TR2 TRACK 86" X 78"

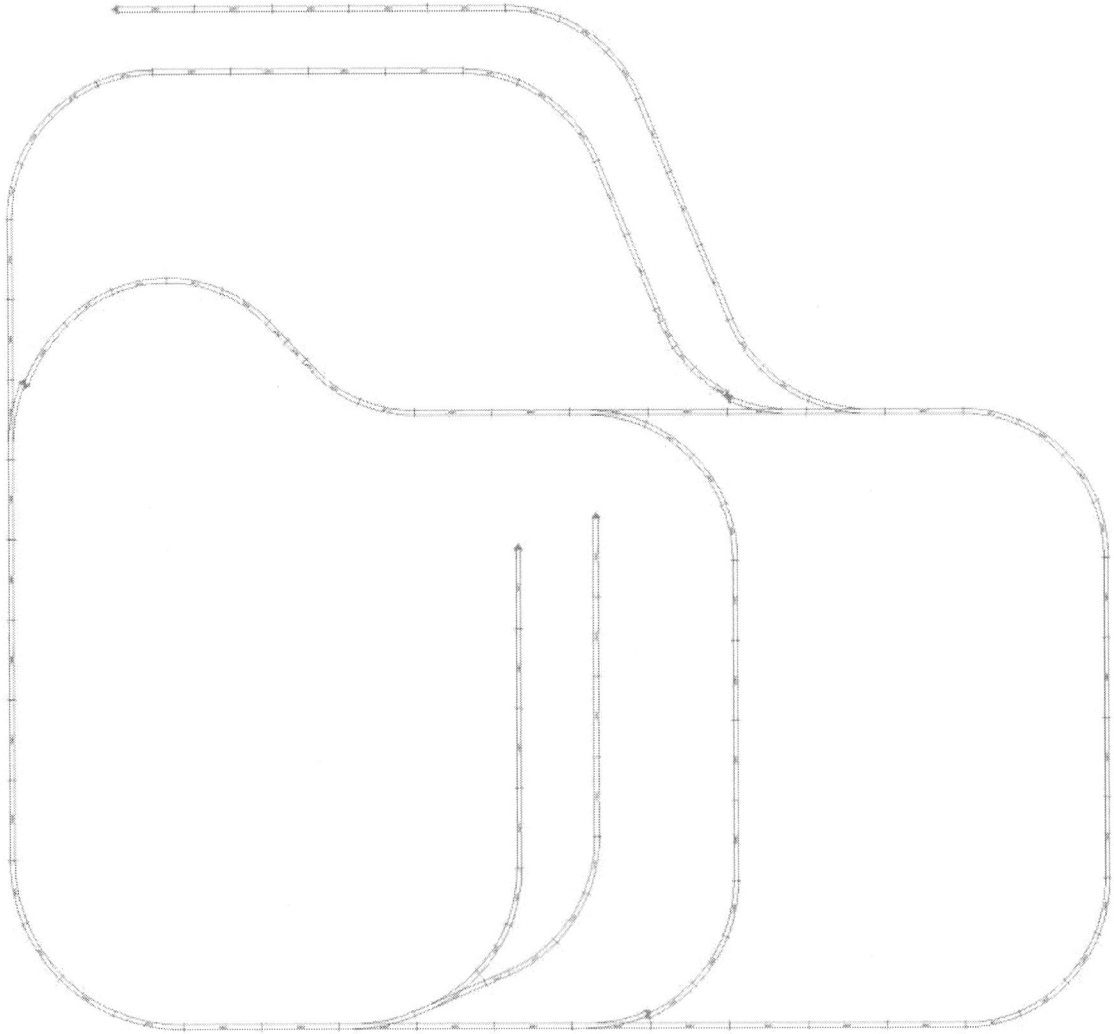

5. N SCALE ATLAS TR2 TRACK 90" X 72"

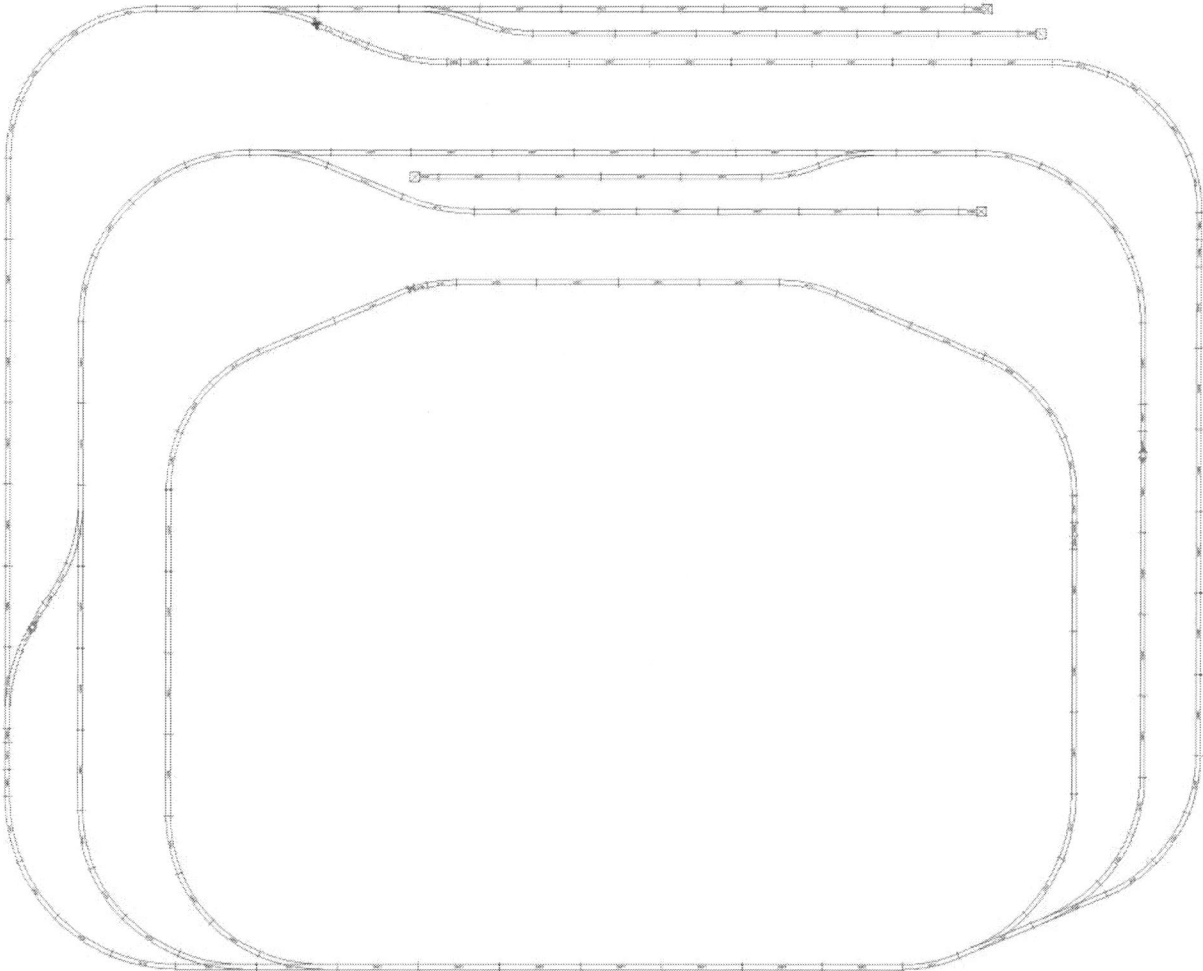

6. N SCALE BACHMANN EZ TRACK NICKEL SILVER 44" X 54"

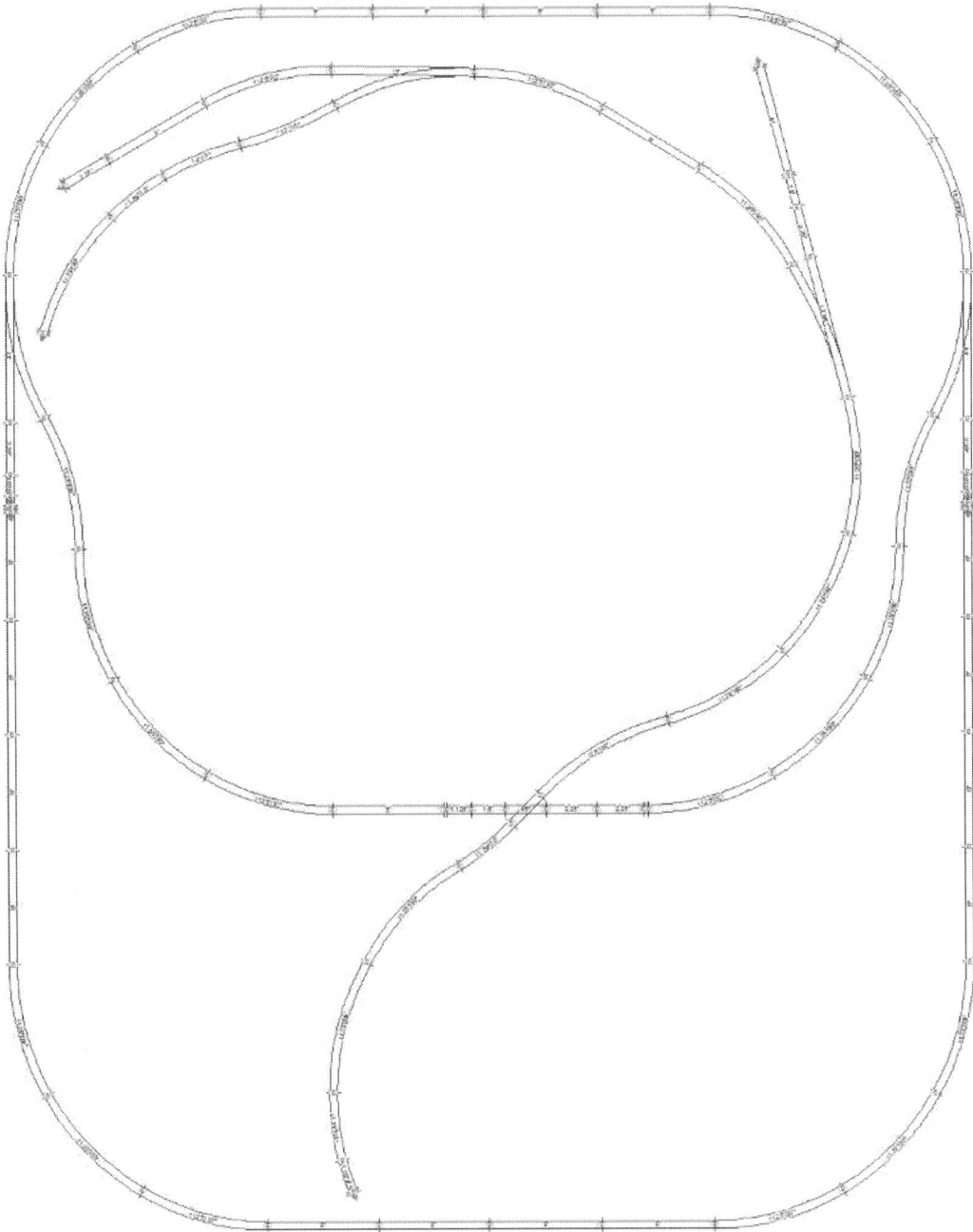

7. N SCALE BACHMANN EZ TRACK NICKEL SILVER 63" X 83"

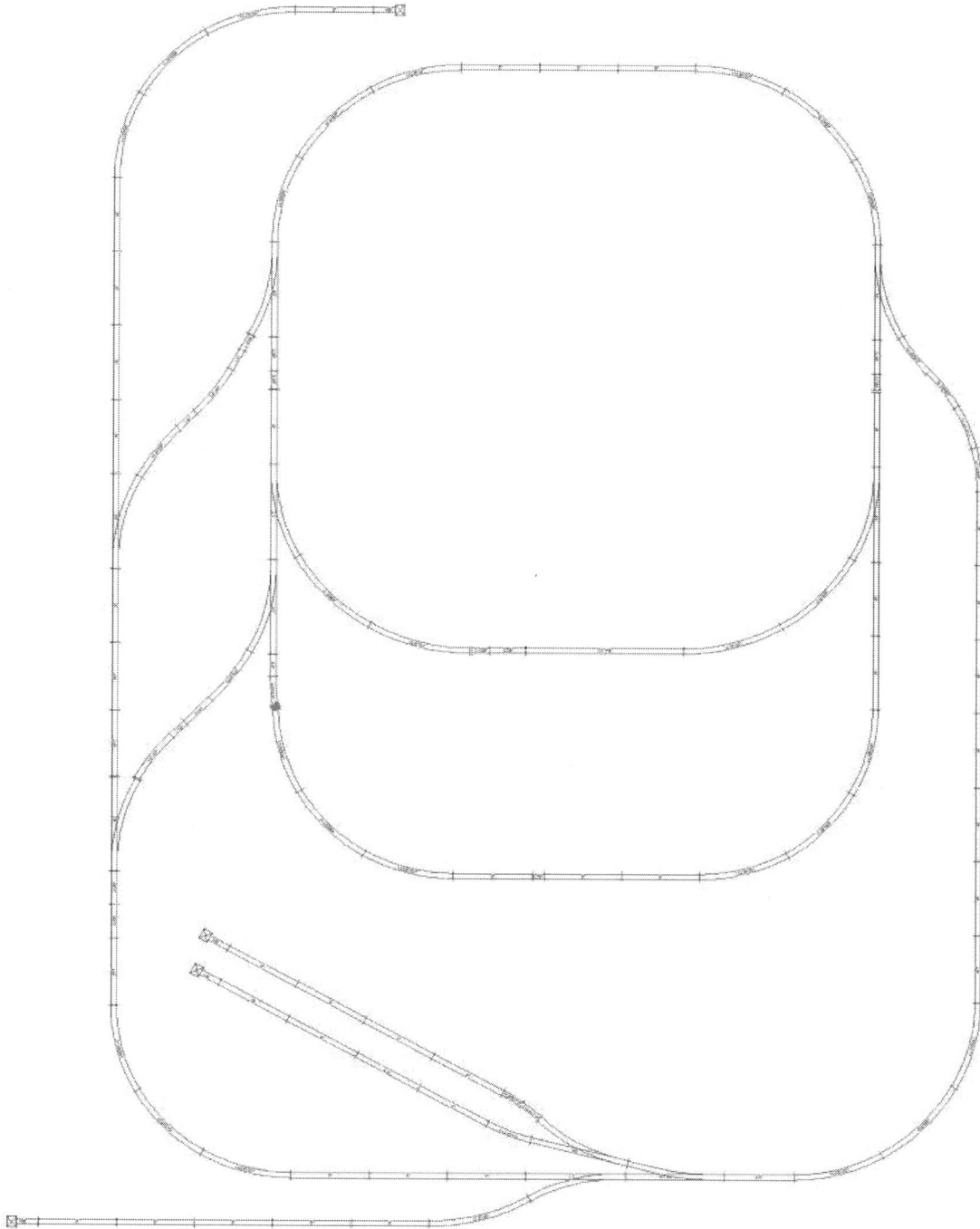

8. Life-Like N Scale Power-loc Track 58" x 46"

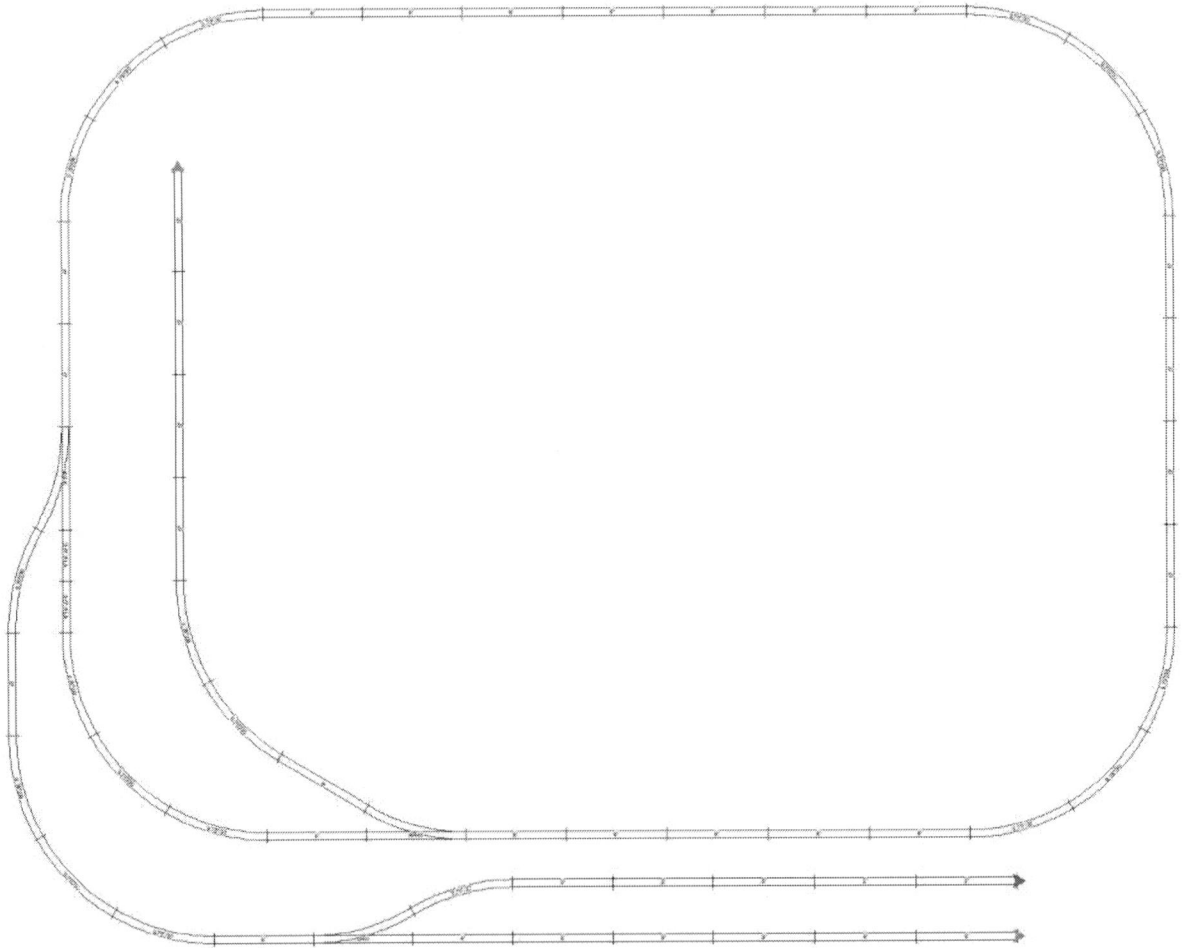

	Part #	Type		Brand	Qty.	
1	7802	5"	N	Walthers	37	
2	7803	9.75"/30	N	Walthers	19	
3	7807	2.5" PLA	N	Walthers	2	Power-Link Adapter
4	7810	RH-R	N	Walthers	1	Remote Switch
5	7810M	RH-M	N	Walthers	1	Manual Switch
6	7811M	LH-M	N	Walthers	1	Manual Switch

Total: 61

9. Bachmann N Scale EZ Track Nickel Silver 122" X 101"

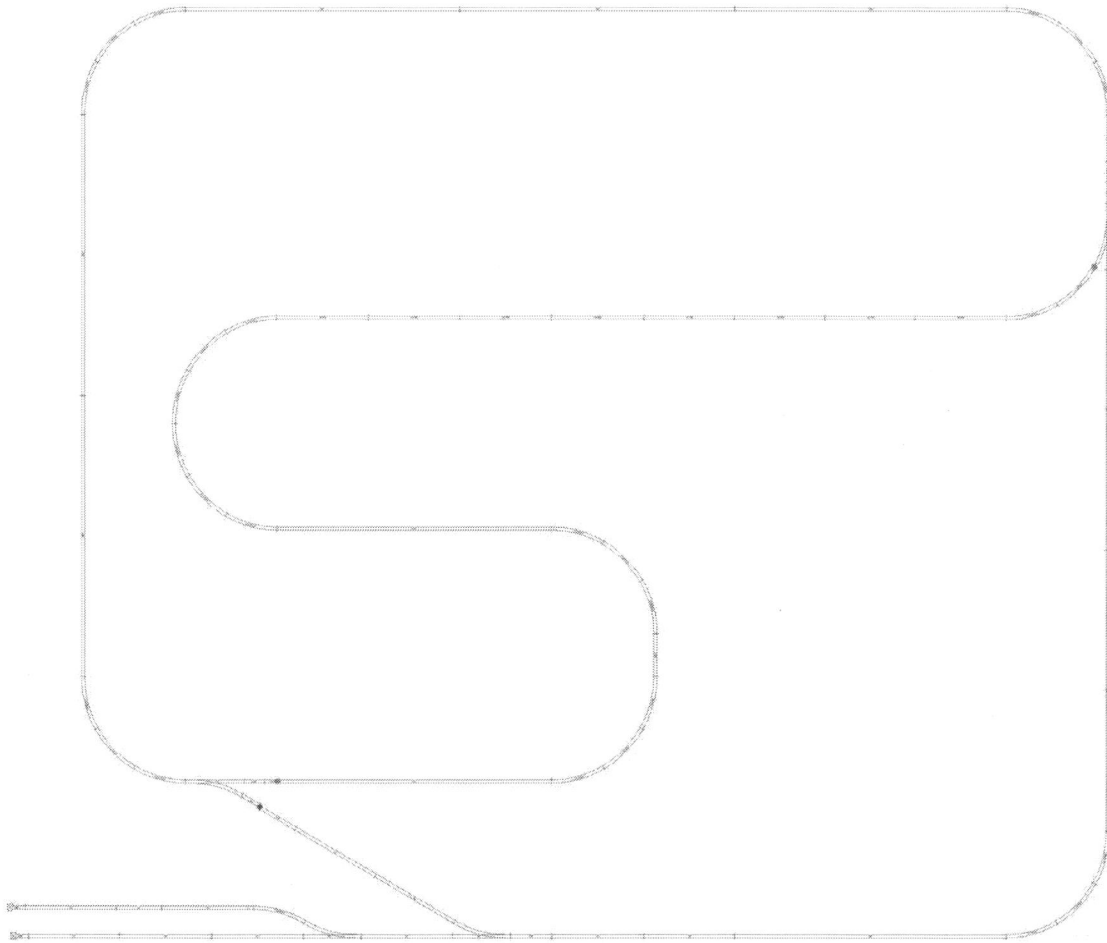

Part #   Type Brand Qty.

	Part #	Type	Brand	Qty.	
1	44801	11.25"/30°	N Bachmann	27	
2	44811	5"	N Bachmann	2	
3	44815	10"	N Bachmann	10	
4	44829a	4.5"	N Bachmann	3	
5	44829b	2.25"	N Bachmann	4	
6	44862	RT	N Bachmann	4	
7	44887	30"	N Bachmann	10	
8	44891	HB	N Bachmann	2	Bumper
9	44897	10" FD	N Bachmann	8	
10	44899a	1.5"	N Bachmann	1	
11	44899d	0.75"	N Bachmann	1	

Total: 72

10. Bachmann N Scale EZ Track Nickel Silver 125" X 109"

	Part #	Type		Brand	Qty	
1	44801	11.25"/30°	N	Bachmann	35	
2	44802	11.25"/30° TR	N	Bachmann	1	
3	44811	5"	N	Bachmann	4	
4	44815	10"	N	Bachmann	18	
5	44829a	4.5"	N	Bachmann	5	
6	44829b	2.25"	N	Bachmann	4	
7	44861	LT	N	Bachmann	1	
8	44862	RT	N	Bachmann	5	
9	44887	30"	N	Bachmann	11	
10	44891	HB	N	Bachmann	4	Bumper
11	44897	10" FD	N	Bachmann	8	
12	44899a	1.5"	N	Bachmann	2	
13	44899d	0.75"	N	Bachmann	2	

Total: 100

11. Life-Like N Scale Power-loc Track 72" x 38"

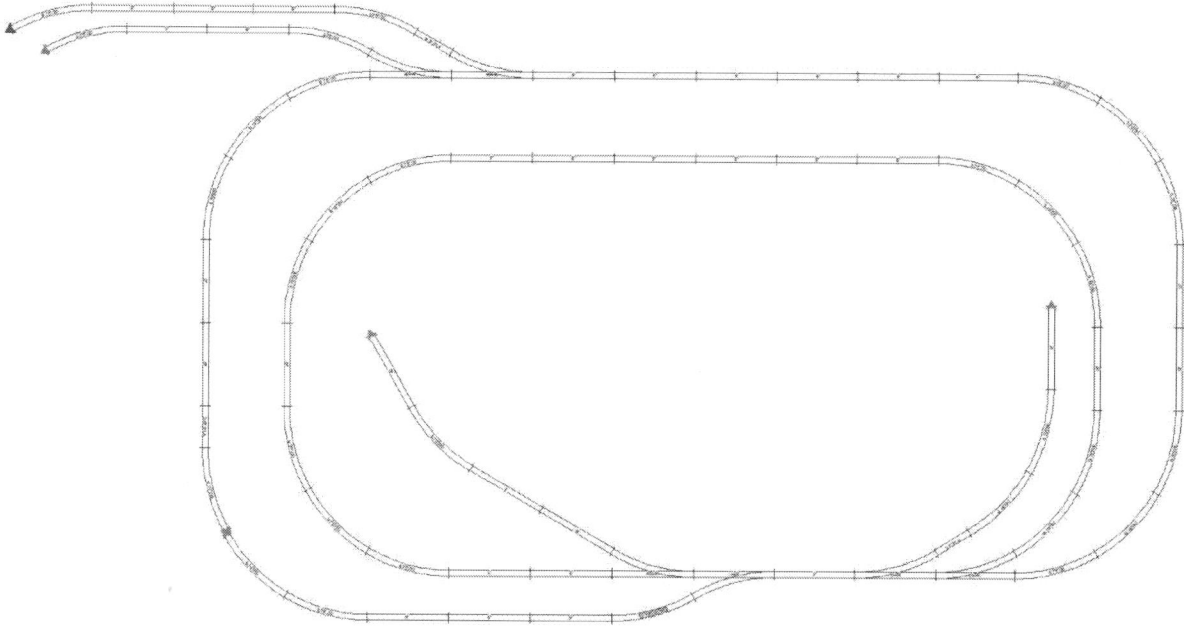

Part #   Type   Brand Qty.

	Part #	Type	Brand	Qty.	
1	7802	5" N	Walthers	33	
2	7803	9.75"/30	N	Walthers	30
3	7806	9.75"/30 TR	N	Walthers	1	Terminal Rerailer
4	7807	2.5" PLA	N	Walthers	3	Power-Link Adapter
5	7810	RH-R N	Walthers	3	Remote Switch
6	7811	LH-R N	Walthers	3	Remote Swit

Total: 73

12. Life-Like N Scale Power-loc Track 77" x 36"

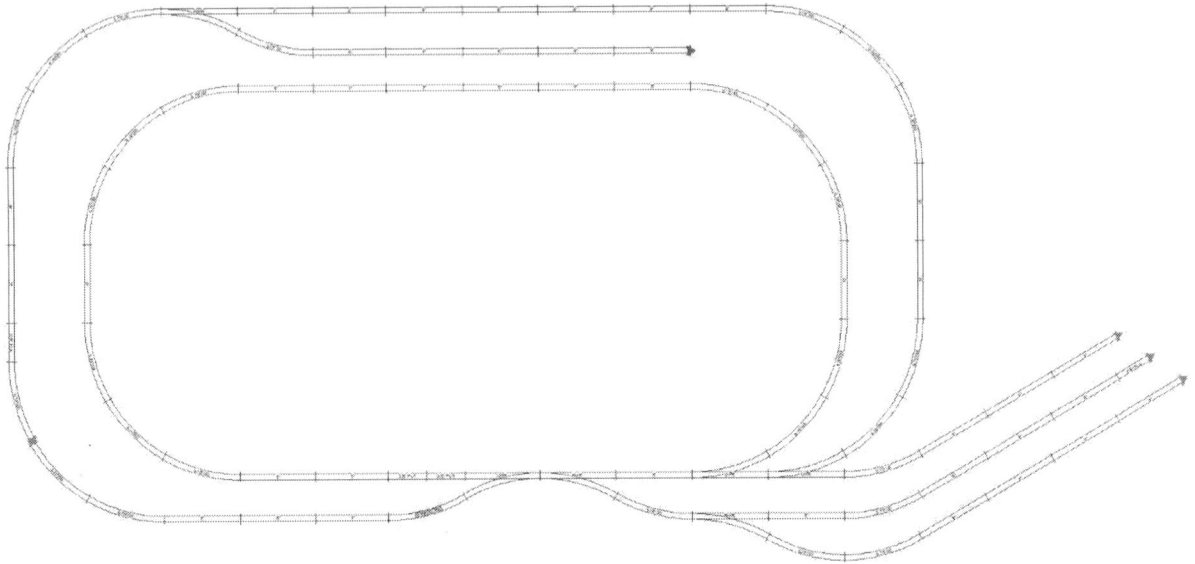

Part #   Type   Brand Qty.

	Part #	Type	Brand	Qty.	
1	7802	5" N	Walthers	41	
2	7803	9.75"/30	N Walthers	28	
3	7806	9.75"/30 TR	N Walthers	1	Terminal Rerailer
4	7807	2.5" PLA	N Walthers	4	Power-Link Adapter
5	7810	RH-R N	Walthers	3	Remote Switch
6	7811	LH-R N	Walthers	3	Remote Switch

Total: 80

13. Life-Like N Scale Power-loc Track 75" x 41"

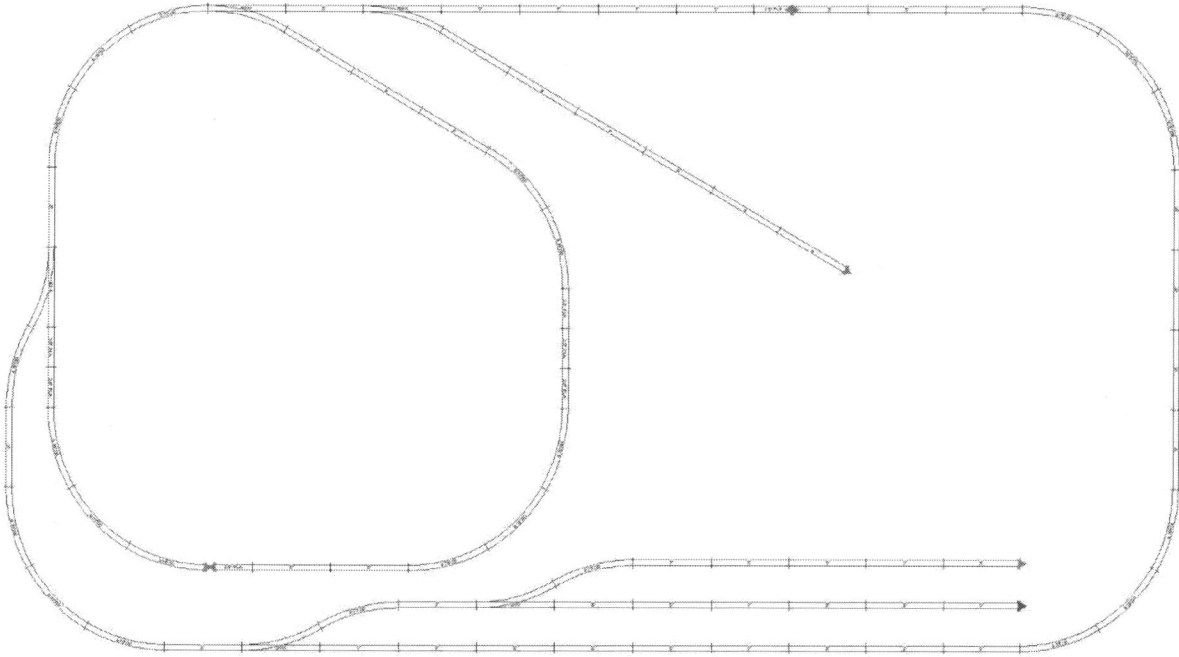

	Part #	Type	Brand	Qty.	
1	7802	5" N	Walthers	47	
2	7803	9.75"/30	N Walthers	23	
3	7807	2.5" PLA	N Walthers	7	Power-Link Adapter
4	7810	RH-R N	Walthers	1	Remote Switch
5	7810M	RH-M N	Walthers	2	Manual Switch
6	7811M	LH-M N	Walthers	2	Manual Switch

Total: 82

14. Life-Like N Scale Power-loc Track 81" x 44"

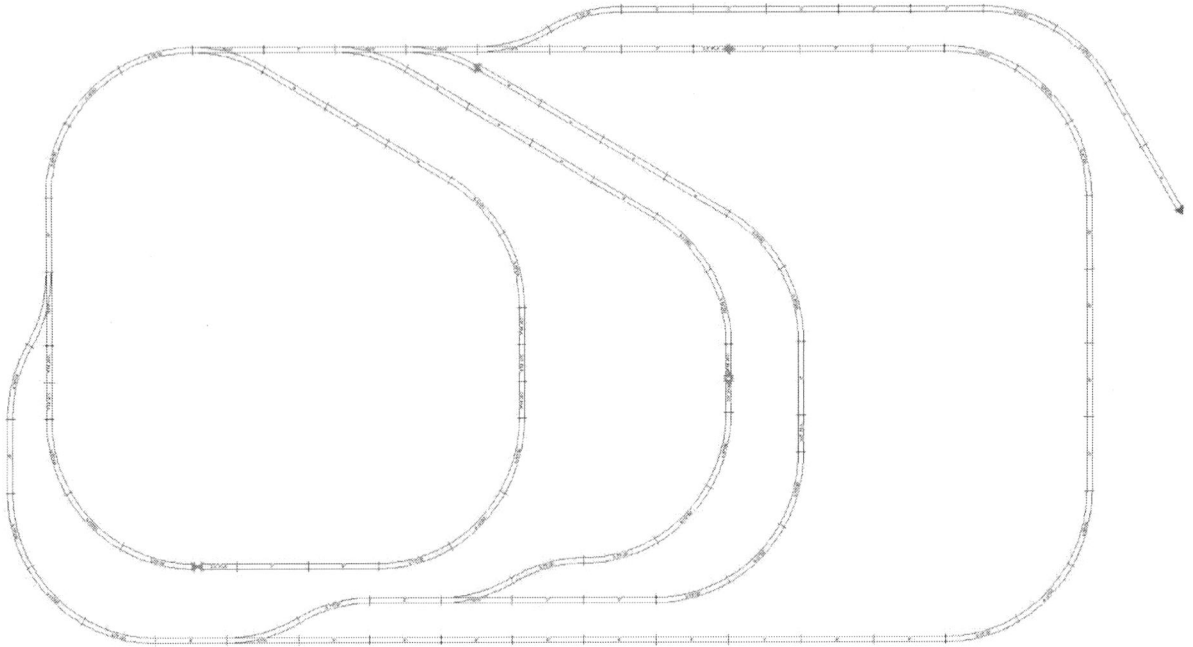

Part #   Type   Brand Qty.

	Part #	Type		Brand	Qty.	
1	7802	5"	N	Walthers	46	
2	7803	9.75"/30	N	Walthers	36	
3	7807	2.5" PLA	N	Walthers	10	Power-Link Adapter
4	7810	RH-R	N	Walthers	1	Remote Switch
5	7810M	RH-M	N	Walthers	3	Manual Switch
6	7811	LH-R	N	Walthers	1	Remote Switch
7	7811M	LH-M	N	Walthers	2	Manual Switch

Total: 99

15. Bachmann N Scale EZ Track Nickel Silver 41" x 74"

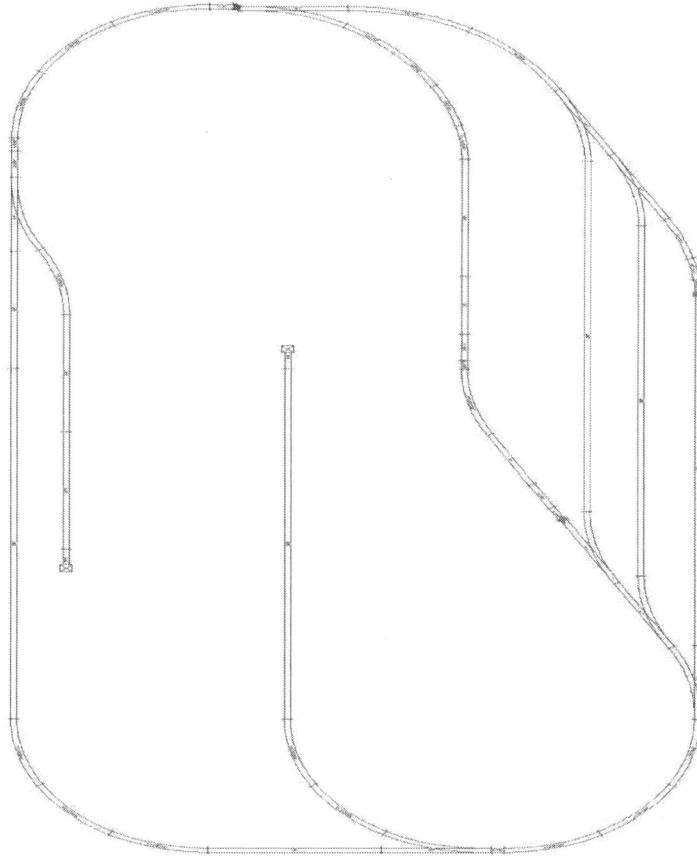

	Part #		Type	Brand	Qty.	
1	44801	11.25"/30°	N	Bachmann	13	
2	44811	5"	N	Bachmann	2	
3	44815	10"	N	Bachmann	5	
4	44821	11.25"/15°	N	Bachmann	1	
5	44823	14"/15°	N	Bachmann	4	
6	44829b	2.25"	N	Bachmann	3	
7	44829c	1.125"	N	Bachmann	1	
8	44833	14"/7.5°	N	Bachmann	1	
9	44836	19"/3.75°	N	Bachmann	1	
10	44853	14"/30°	N	Bachmann	2	
11	44861	LT	N	Bachmann	2	
12	44862	RT	N	Bachmann	6	
13	44887	30"	N	Bachmann	5	
14	44891	HB	N	Bachmann	2	Bumper
15	44899a	1.5"	N	Bachmann	1	
16	44899b	1.25"	N	Bachmann	1	
17	44899d	0.75"	N	Bachmann	2	

Total: 52

16. Bachmann N Scale EZ Track Nickel Silver 51" x 74"

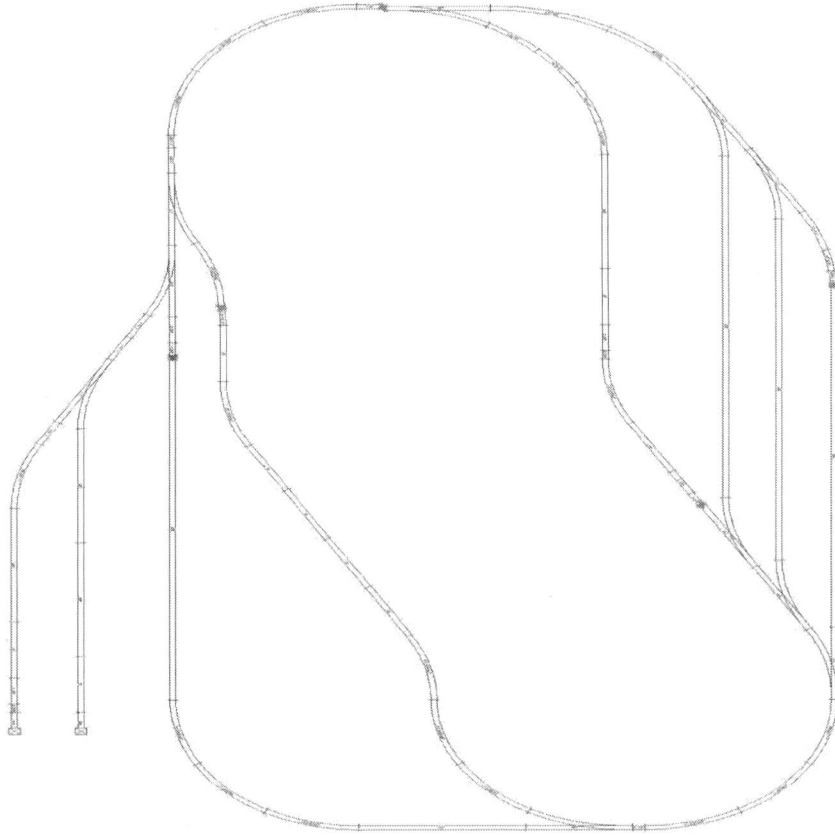

	Part #	Type		Brand	Qty.	
1	44801	11.25"/30°	N	Bachmann	16	
2	44811	5"	N	Bachmann	8	
3	44815	10"	N	Bachmann	5	
4	44821	11.25"/15°	N	Bachmann	1	
5	44823	14"/15°	N	Bachmann	4	
6	44829a	4.5"	N	Bachmann	1	
7	44829b	2.25"	N	Bachmann	8	
8	44829c	1.125"	N	Bachmann	1	
9	44831	11.25"/7.5°	N	Bachmann	1	
10	44833	14"/7.5°	N	Bachmann	1	
11	44836	19"/3.75°	N	Bachmann	1	
12	44853	14"/30°	N	Bachmann	2	
13	44861	LT	N	Bachmann	3	
14	44862	RT	N	Bachmann	7	
15	44887	30"	N	Bachmann	4	
16	44891	HB	N	Bachmann	2	Bumper
17	44899a	1.5"	N	Bachmann	1	
18	44899b	1.25"	N	Bachmann	2	
19	44899d	0.75"	N	Bachmann	3	

Total: 71

17. Bachmann N Scale EZ Track Nickel Silver 53" x 84"

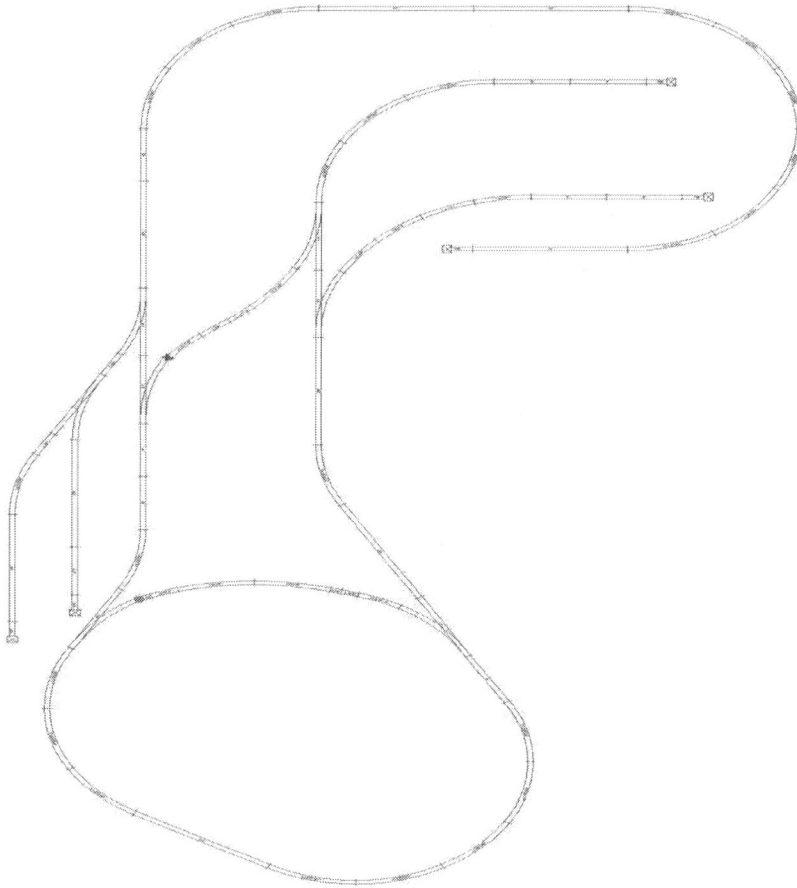

Part #   Type   Brand Qty.

	Part #		Type	Brand	Qty.	
1	44801	11.25"/30°	N	Bachmann	23	
2	44804	19"/15°	N	Bachmann	2	
3	44811	5"	N	Bachmann	8	
4	44815	10"	N	Bachmann	9	
5	44821	11.25"/15°	N	Bachmann	2	
6	44823	14"/15°	N	Bachmann	4	
7	44829a	4.5"	N	Bachmann	1	
8	44829b	2.25"	N	Bachmann	3	
9	44829c	1.125"	N	Bachmann	1	
10	44833	14"/7.5°	N	Bachmann	1	
11	44834	15.5"/7.5°	N	Bachmann	1	
12	44855	17.5"/15°	N	Bachmann	1	
13	44861	LT	N	Bachmann	2	
14	44862	RT	N	Bachmann	5	
15	44891	HB	N	Bachmann	5	Bumper
16	44899c	0.875"	N	Bachmann	1	
17	44899d	0.75"	N	Bachmann	1	

Total: 70

18. Life-Like N Scale Power-loc 46" x 97"

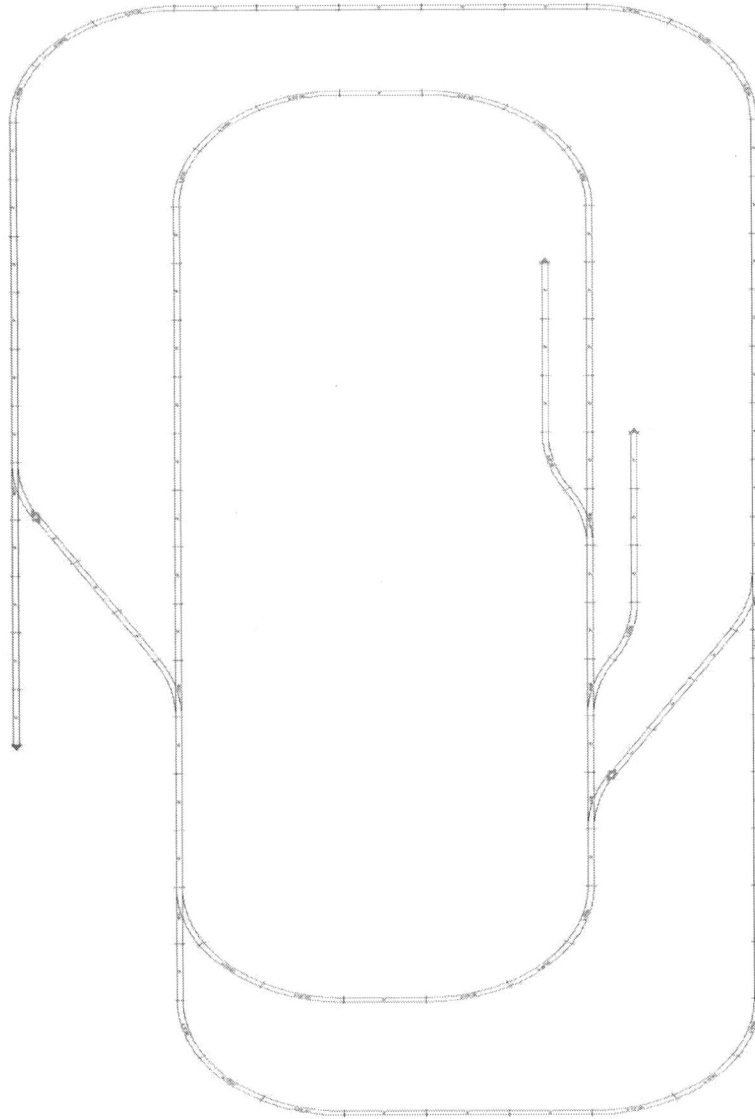

	Part #		Type	Brand	Qty.	
1	7802	5"	N	Walthers	67	
2	7803	9.75"/30	N	Walthers	25	
3	7807	2.5" PLA	N	Walthers	1	Power-Link Adapter
4	7810M	RH-M	N	Walthers	3	Manual Switch
5	7811M	LH-M	N	Walthers	4	Manual Switch
Total:	100					

19. Life-Like N Scale Power-loc 89" x 19"

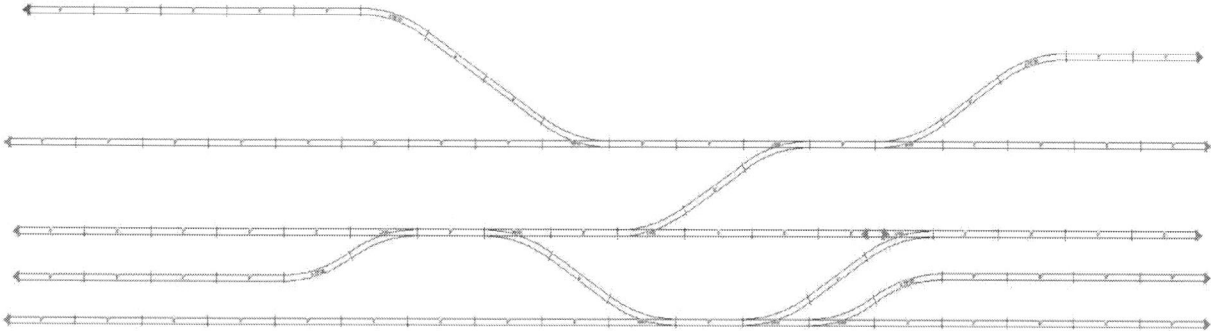

	Part #		Type	Brand	Qty.	
1	7802	5"	N	Walthers	65	
2	7803	9.75"/30	N	Walthers	4	
3	7810M	RH-M	N	Walthers	3	Manual Switch
4	7811	LH-R	N	Walthers	1	Remote Switch
5	7811M	LH-M	N	Walthers	6	Manual Switch
Total:	79					

20. Trix N Scale Track 45" x 59"

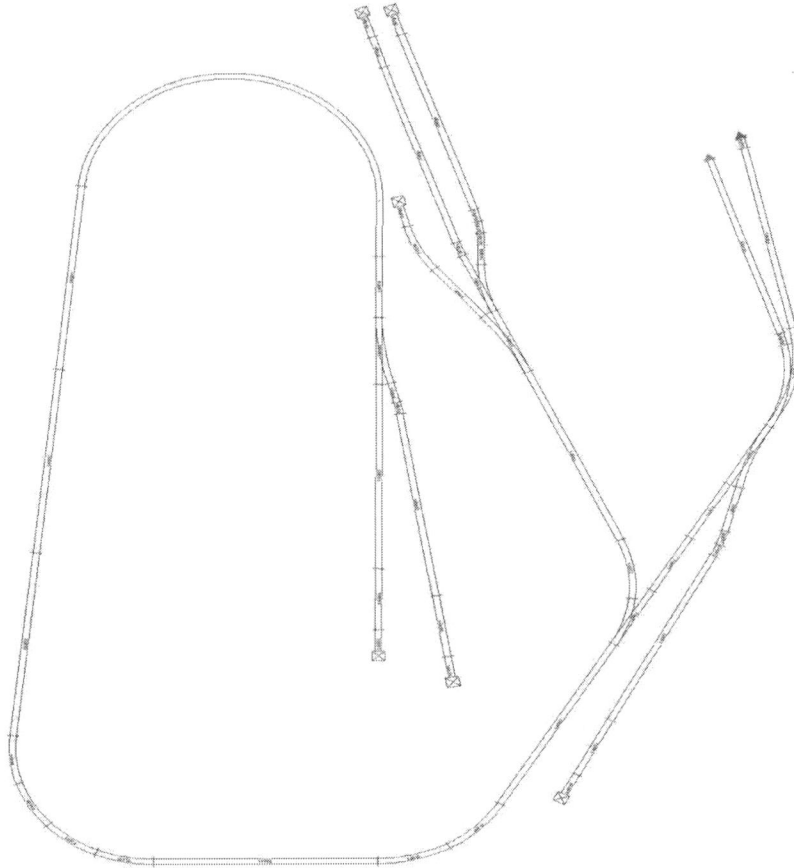

	Part #		Type	Brand	Qty.	
1	14901	14901/Flex	N	Trix	1	
2	14902	14902	N	Trix	13	
3	14904	14904	N	Trix	7	
4	14905	14905	N	Trix	1	
5	14906	14906	N	Trix	1	
6	14909	14909	N	Trix	2	
7	14912	14912	N	Trix	2	
8	14914	14914	N	Trix	5	
9	14916	14916	N	Trix	7	
10	14926	14926	N	Trix	2	
11	14938	14938	N	Trix	1	
12	14954	14954	N	Trix	2	
13	14961	14961	N	Trix	1	
14	14963	14963	N	Trix	1	
15	14966	14966	N	Trix	1	
16	14972	14972	N	Trix	1	Feeder track
17	14976	14976	N	Trix	6	Bumper

Total: 54

21. Trix N Scale Track 49" x 93"

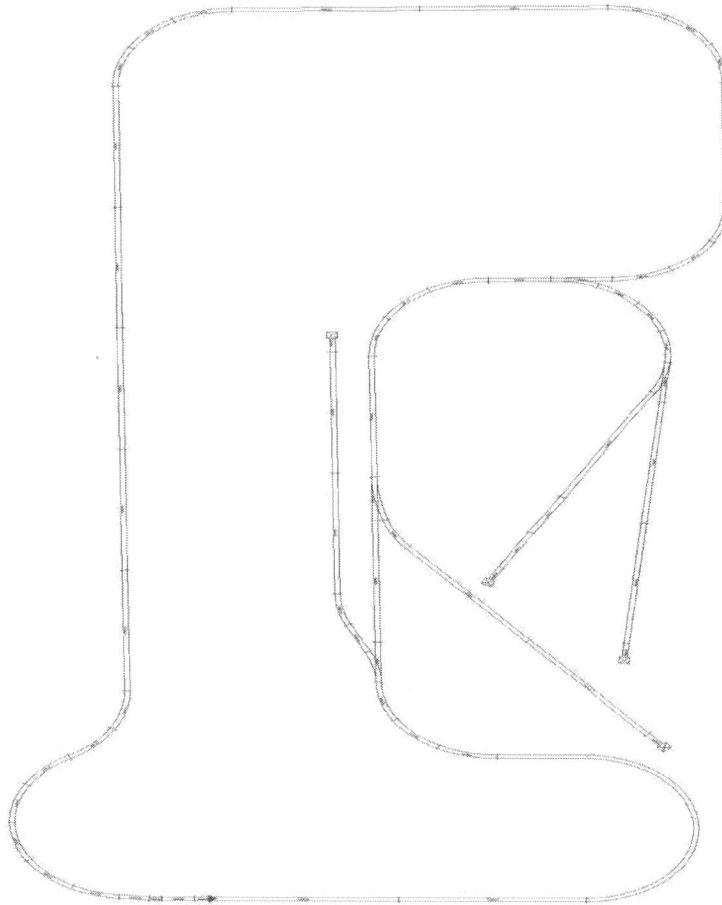

	Part #		Type	Brand	Qty.	
1	14901	14901/Flex	N	Trix	1	
2	14902	14902	N	Trix	19	
3	14904	14904	N	Trix	3	
4	14905	14905	N	Trix	1	
5	14906	14906	N	Trix	1	
6	14907	14907	N	Trix	1	
7	14908	14908	N	Trix	1	
8	14912	14912	N	Trix	21	
9	14914	14914	N	Trix	3	
10	14916	14916	N	Trix	1	
11	14954	14954	N	Trix	1	
12	14961	14961	N	Trix	1	
13	14963	14963	N	Trix	2	
14	14976	14976	N	Trix	4	Bumper
15	14984	14984	N	Trix	3	Double Isolation track

Total: 63

22. Trix N Scale Track 57" x 85"

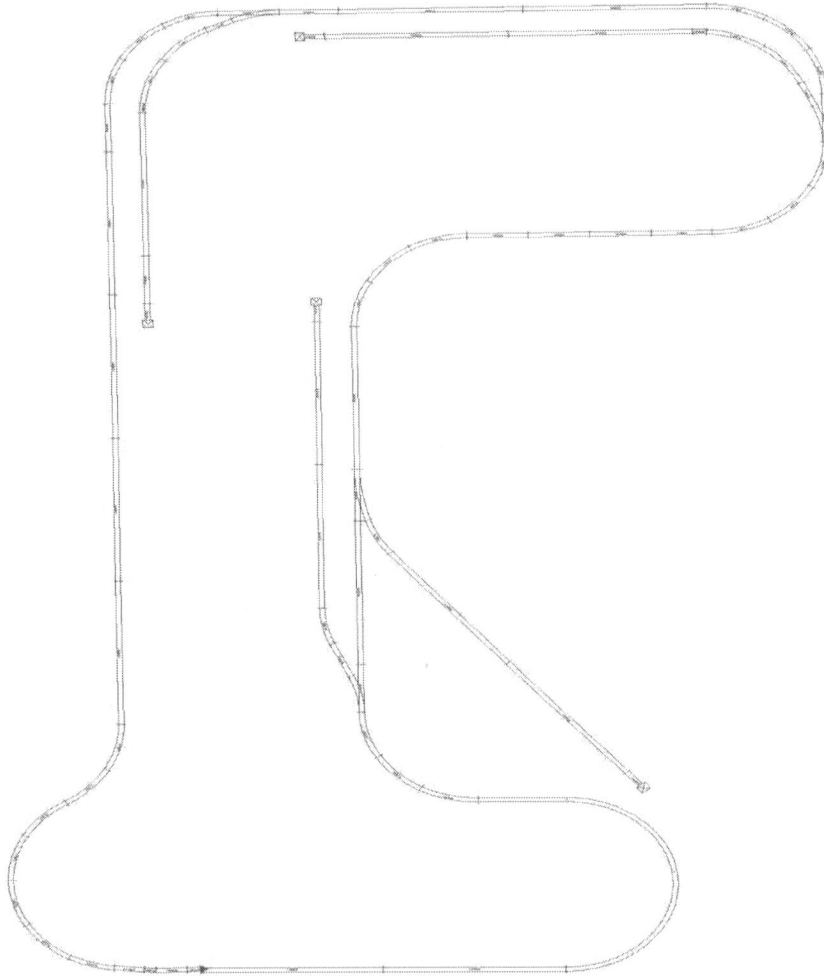

	Part #		Type	Brand	Qty.	
1	14901	14901/Flex	N	Trix	1	
2	14902	14902	N	Trix	17	
3	14904	14904	N	Trix	7	
4	14905	14905	N	Trix	1	
5	14906	14906	N	Trix	2	
6	14907	14907	N	Trix	2	
7	14908	14908	N	Trix	1	
8	14912	14912	N	Trix	25	
9	14914	14914	N	Trix	3	
10	14916	14916	N	Trix	2	
11	14926	14926	N	Trix	1	
12	14951	14951	N	Trix	1	
13	14954	14954	N	Trix	1	
14	14961	14961	N	Trix	2	
15	14976	14976	N	Trix	4	Bumper

Total: 70

23. HO SCALE ATLAS TR2 TRACK 93" X 71"

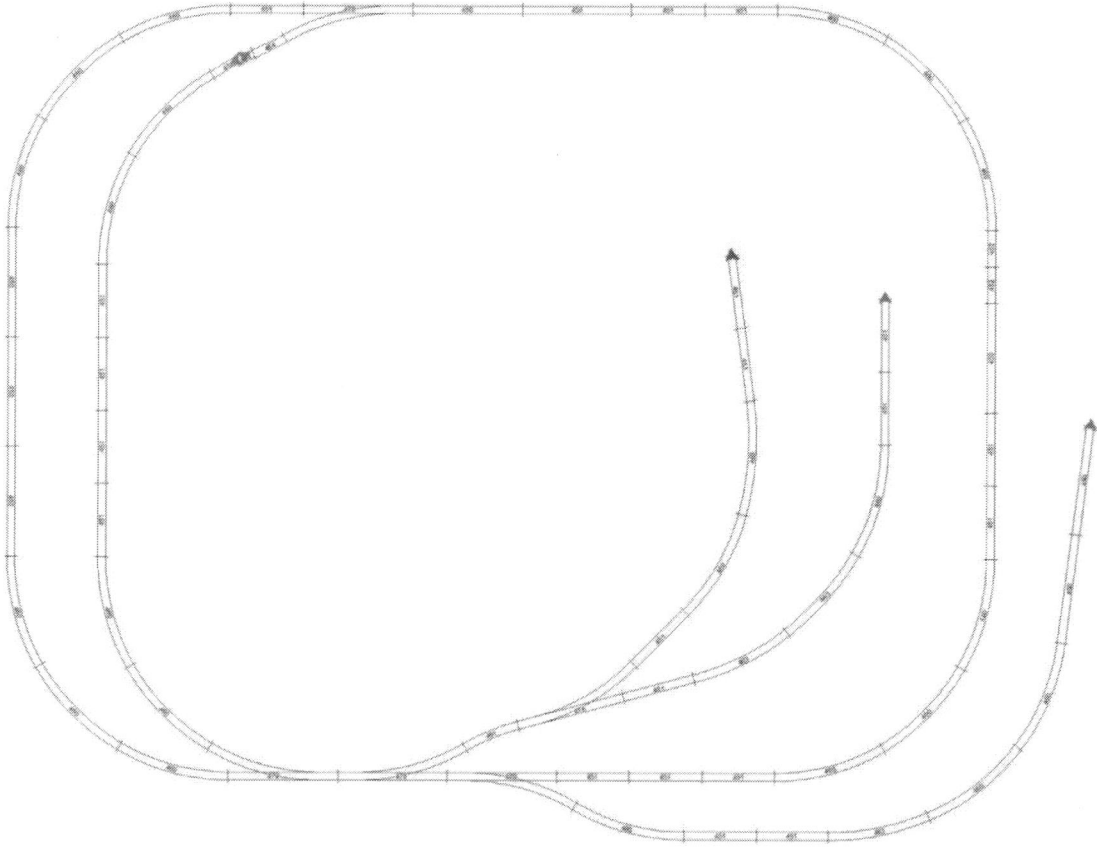

24. HO SCALE ATLAS TR2 TRACK 121" X 59"

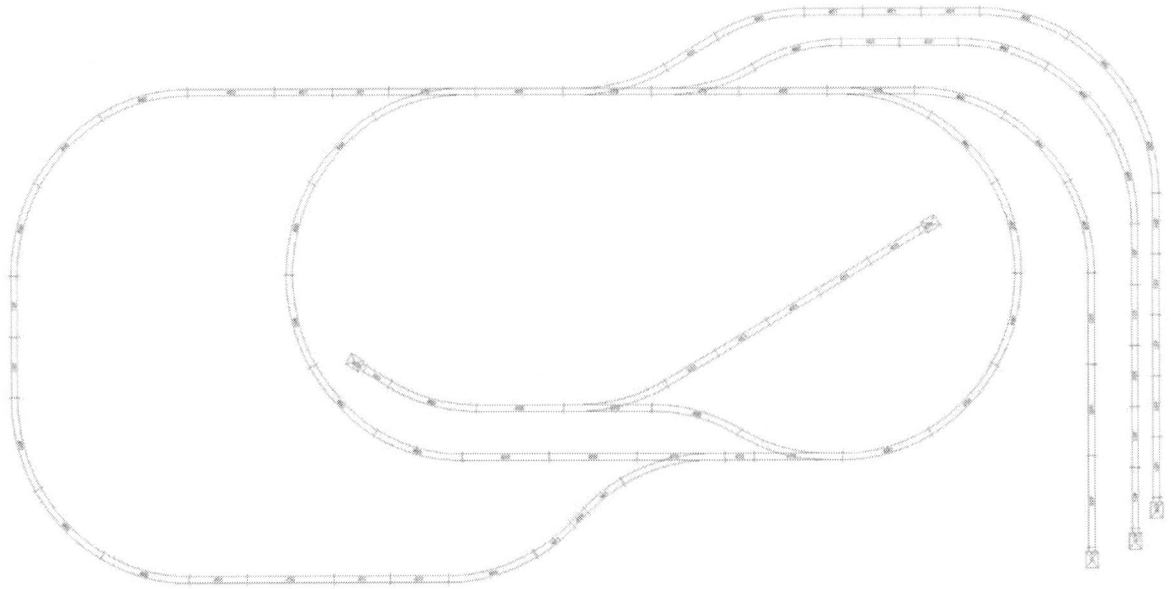

25. HO SCALE ATLAS TRUE TRACK 61" X 99"

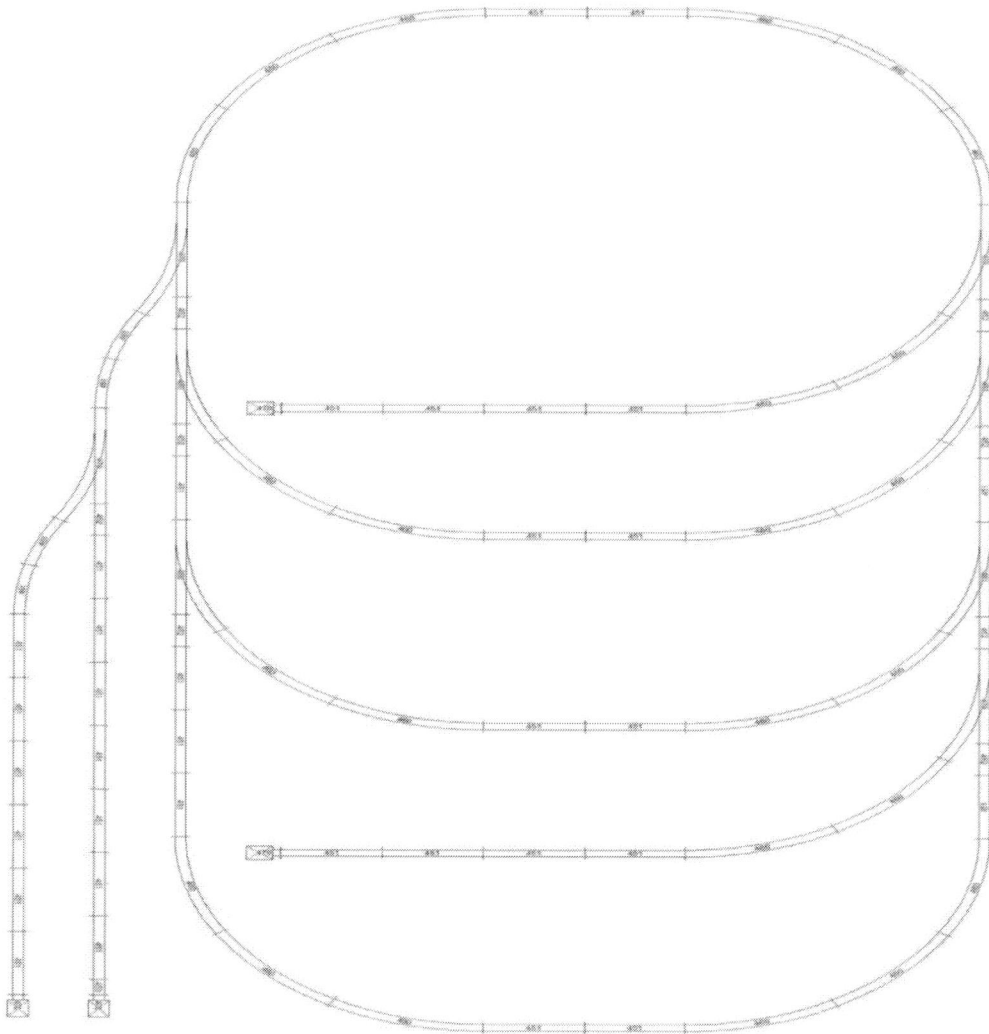

26. HO SCALE ATLAS TRUE TRACK 62" X 125"

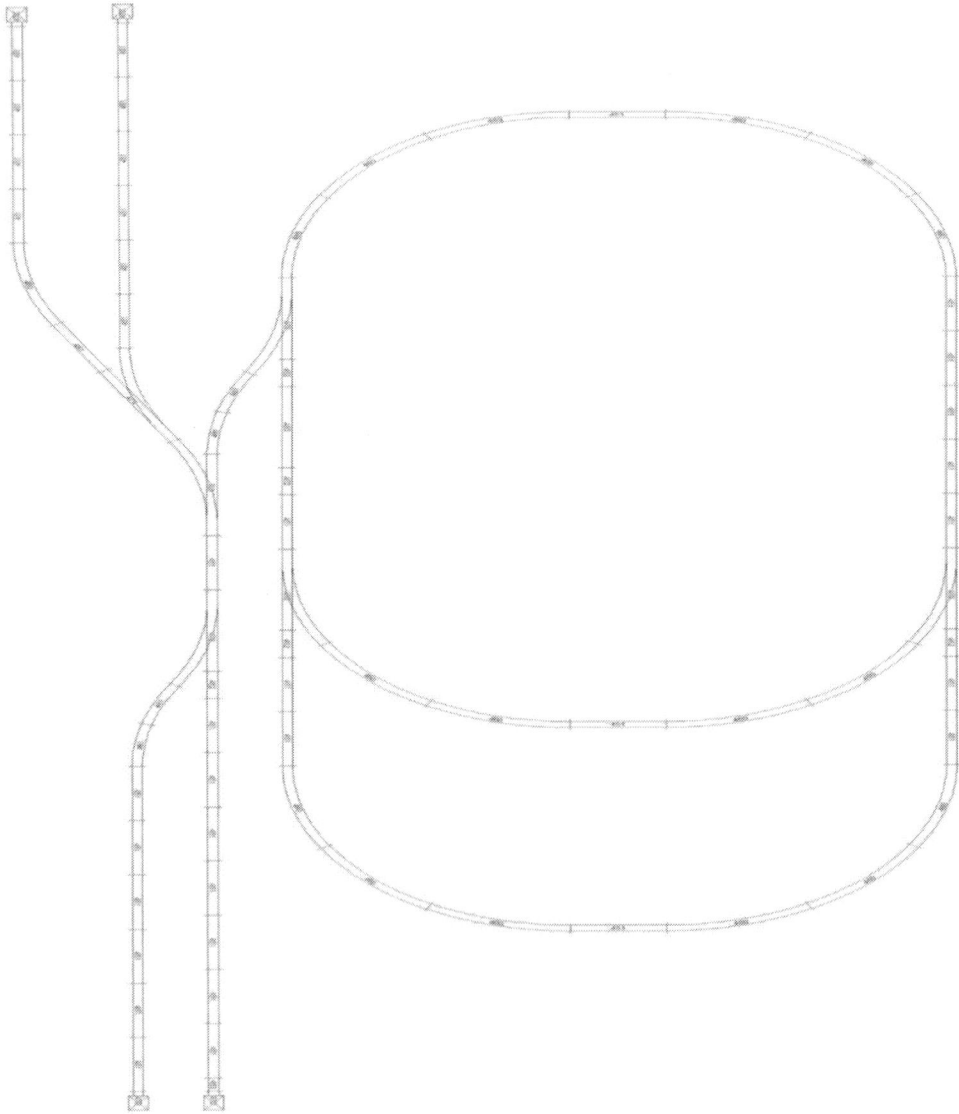

27.   HO SCALE ATLAS TRUE TRACK 83" X 96"

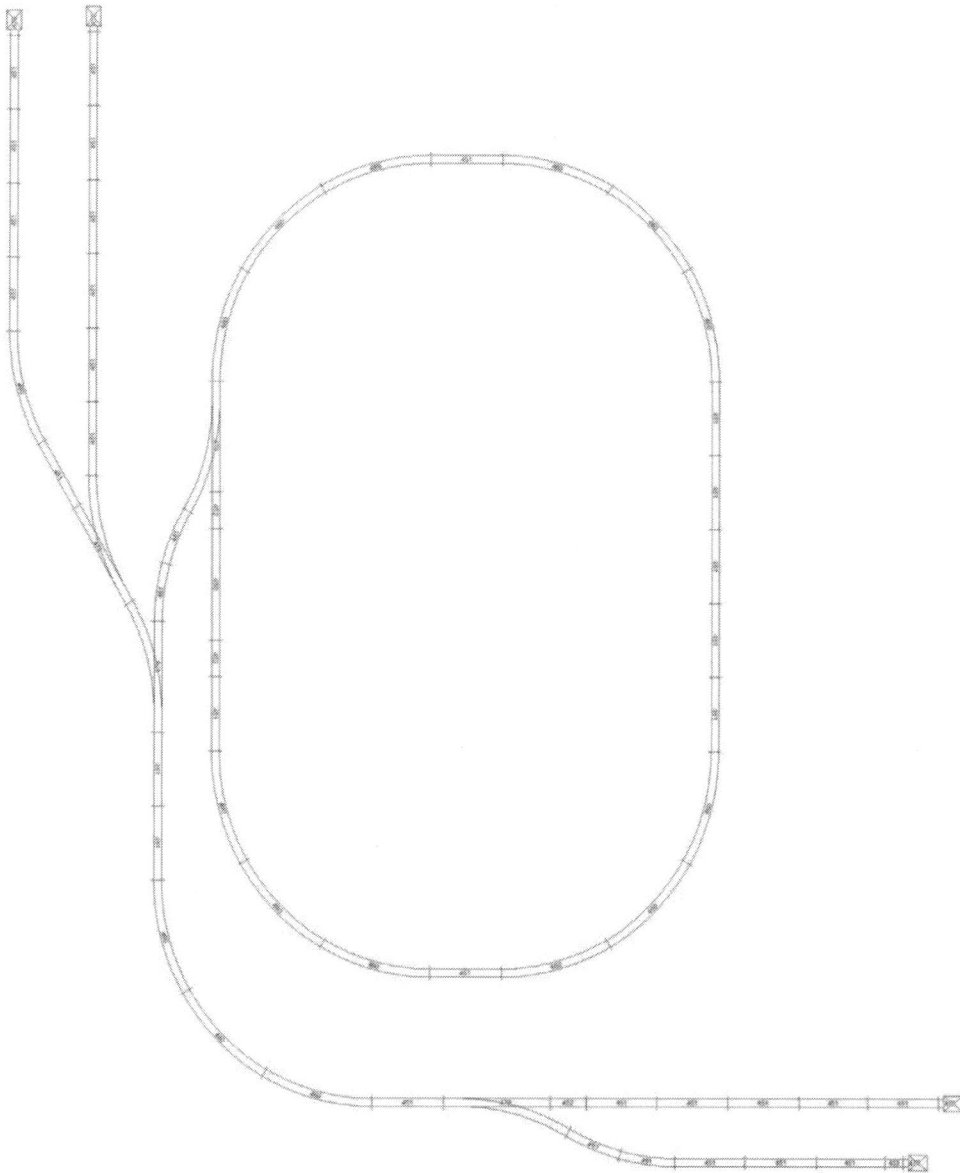

28. HO SCALE ATLAS TRUE TRACK 105" X 114"

29. HO SCALE BACHMANN EZ TRACK NICKEL SILVER 84" X 93"

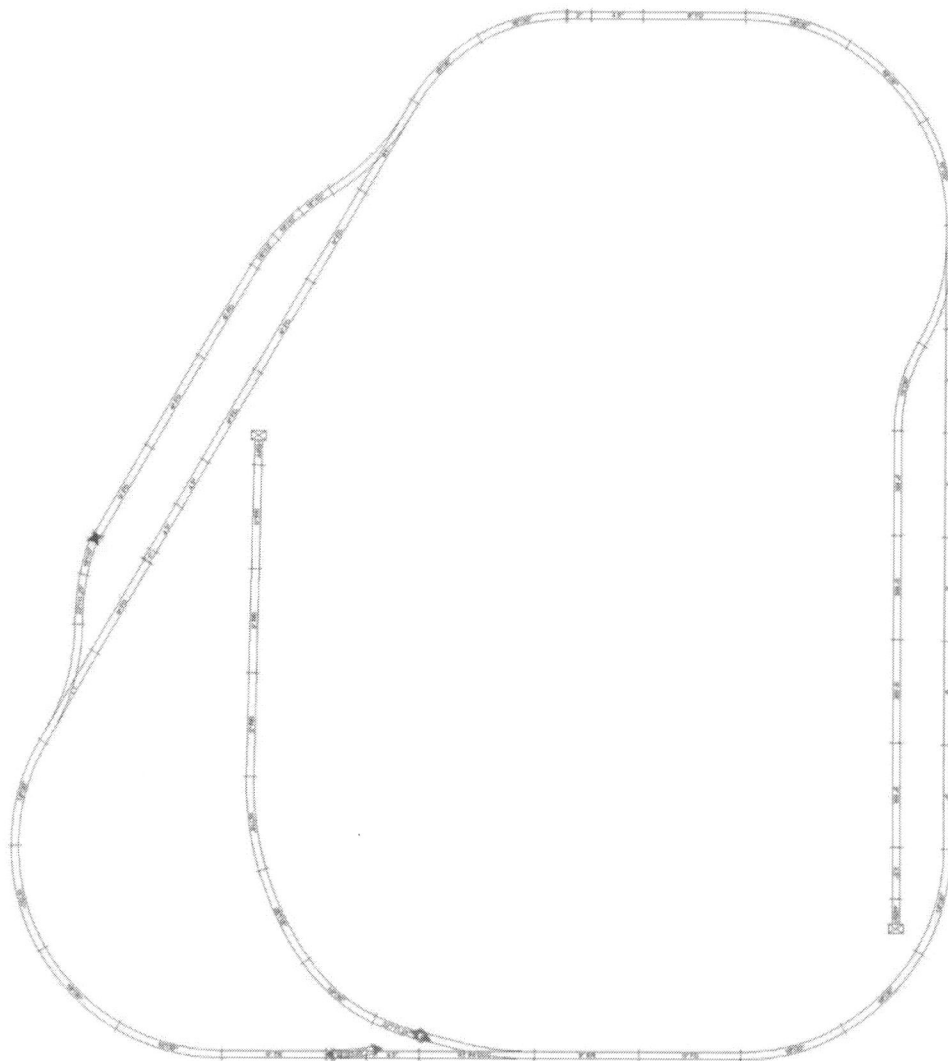

30. HO SCALE BACHMANN EZ TRACK NICKEL SILVER 106" X 102"

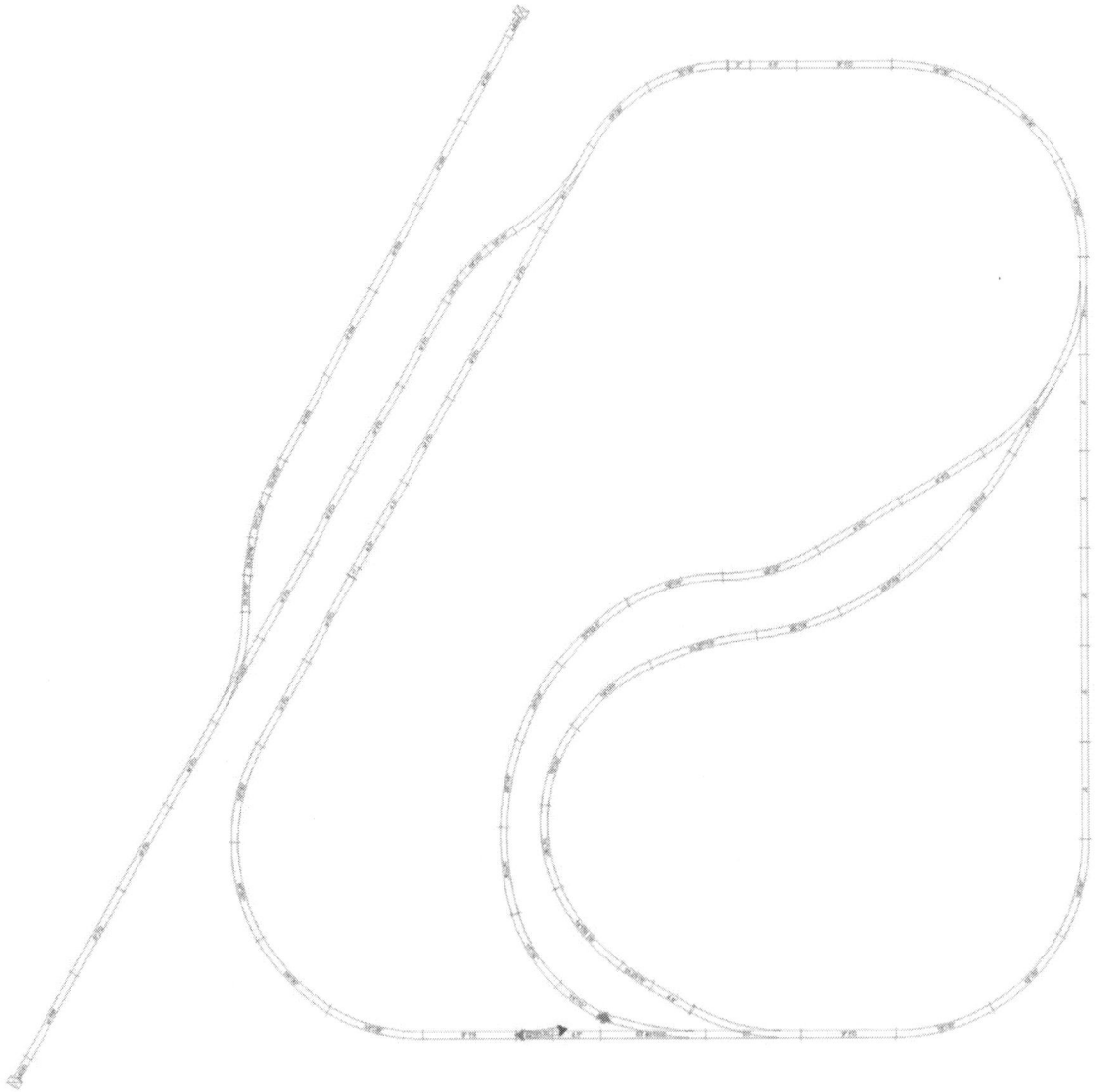

31. Kato HO Scale Uni-Track 211" x 52"

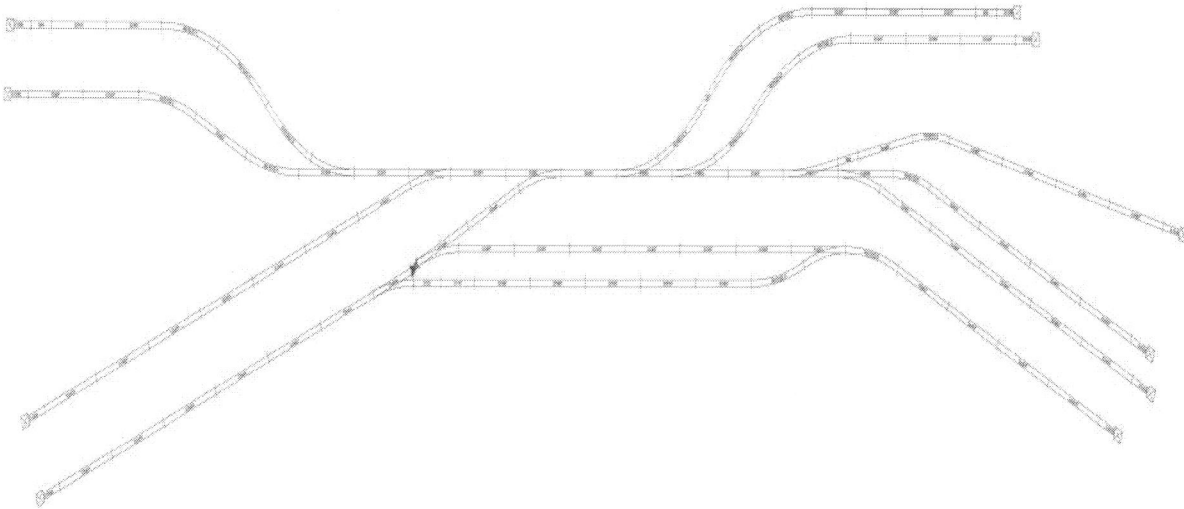

Part #   Type Brand Qty.

	Part #	Type		Brand	Qty.	
1	2-111	S94	HO	Kato	3	
2	2-140	S123	HO	Kato	1	
3	2-151	S246F	HO	Kato	58	Straight Feeder
4	2-170	S109B	HO	Kato	10	Track End
5	2-193	S149	HO	Kato	1	
6	2-210	R550/22,5		HO	Kato	2
7	2-220	R610/22,5		HO	Kato	8
8	2-230	R670/22,5		HO	Kato	3
9	2-260	R430/22,5		HO	Kato	2
10	2-840	P490L	HO	Kato	4	
11	2-841	P490R	HO	Kato	3	
12	2-850	P550L	HO	Kato	1	
13	2-851	P550R	HO	Kato	1	
14	2-860	P867L	HO	Kato	1	
15	97	S97	HO	Kato	1	

Total: 99

32. Life-Like HO Scale Power-loc Nickel Silver Track 139" x 94"

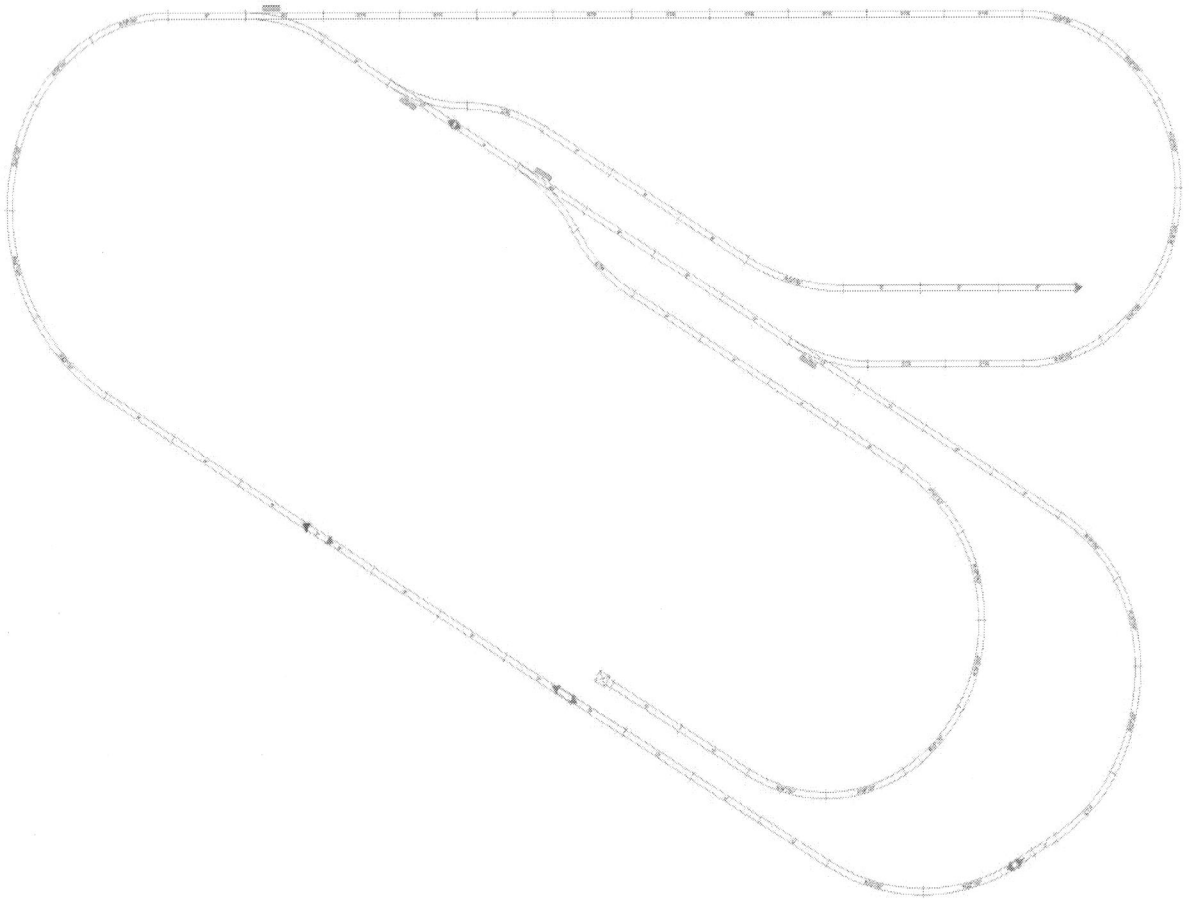

Part #   Type   Brand Qty.

	Part #	Type	Brand	Qty.	
1	21332	9"	HO	Walthers	33	
2	21333	R18"/30°	HO	Walthers	16	
3	21334	CTR	HO	Walthers	3	Curved Terminal Rerailer
4	21335	LT	HO	Walthers	2	Remote Turnout
5	21336	RT	HO	Walthers	2	Remote Turnout
6	21347	3"	HO	Walthers	3	
7	21348	R22"/30°	HO	Walthers	7	
8	21394	STR	HO	Walthers	10	Straight Terminal Rerailer

Total: 76

33. Life-Like HO Scale Power-loc Track Steel 76" x 114"

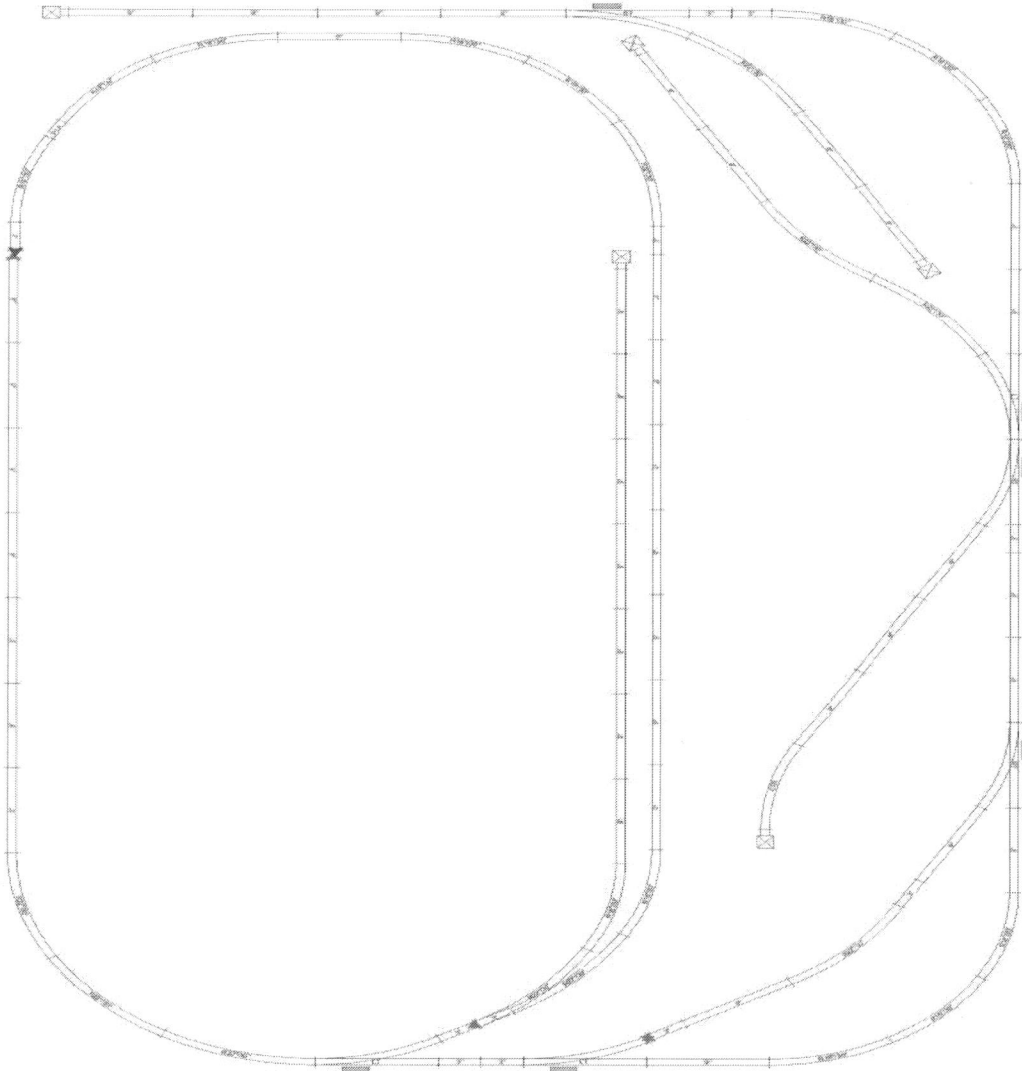

Part #   Type   Brand Qty.

	Part #	Type	Brand	Qty.	
1	21302	9"	HO	Walthers	41
2	21303	R18"/30°	HO	Walthers	13
3	21304	CTR	HO	Walthers	1	Curved Terminal Rerailer
4	21305	LT	HO	Walthers	3	Remote Turnout
5	21306	RT	HO	Walthers	3	Remote Turnout
6	21308	Bmp	HO	Walthers	5	Bumper
7	21314	PLA	HO	Walthers	1	Power-Link Adapter track
8	21317	3"	HO	Walthers	11	
9	21318	R22"/30°	HO	Walthers	10	

Total: 88

34. Life-Like HO Scale Power-loc Track Steel 84" x 133"

	Part #		Type	Brand	Qty.	
1	21302	9"	HO	Walthers	47	
2	21303	R18"/30°	HO	Walthers	19	
3	21304	CTR	HO	Walthers	2	Curved Terminal Rerailer
4	21305	LT	HO	Walthers	8	Remote Turnout
5	21306	RT	HO	Walthers	2	Remote Turnout
6	21308	Bmp	HO	Walthers	5	Bumper
7	21314	PLA	HO	Walthers	2	Power-Link Adapter track
8	21317	3"	HO	Walthers	11	
9	21318	R22"/30°	HO	Walthers	4	

Total: 100

35. Atlas HO Scale TR2 Track 144" x 17"

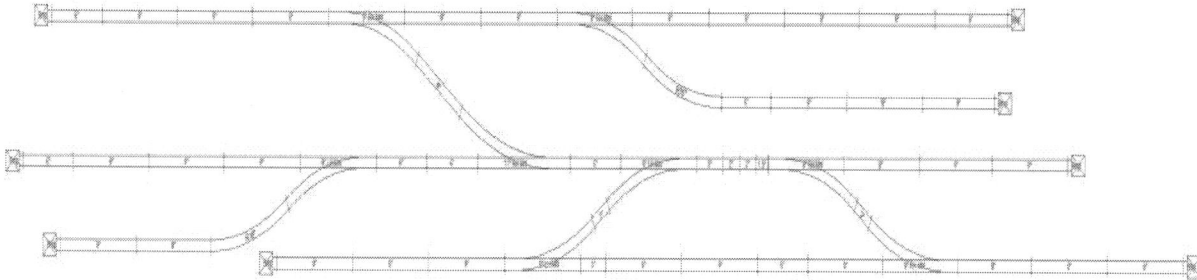

	Part #	Type	Brand	Qty.		
1	450	9"	HO	Atlas	30	
2	451	6"	HO	Atlas	8	
3	452	3"	HO	Atlas	2	
4	453	1.5"	HO	Atlas	1	
5	454	2"	HO	Atlas	4	
6	460	R18"	HO	Atlas	2	
7	470	Bmp	HO	Atlas	8	Bumper
8	478	9" LH Mnl	HO	Atlas	3	9" Manual Snap Switch
9	479	9" RH Mnl	HO	Atlas	4	9" Manual Snap Switch
10	483	11" RH Mnl	HO	Atlas	1	11" Manual Snap Switch
Total:	63					

36. Bachmann HO Scale EZ Track Nickel Silver 125" x 109"

Part #   Type   Brand   Qty.

	Part #	Type	Brand	Qty.	
1	44801	11.25"/30°	N	Bachmann	35
2	44802	11.25"/30° TR	N	Bachmann	1
3	44811	5"	N	Bachmann	4
4	44815	10"	N	Bachmann	18
5	44829a	4.5"	N	Bachmann	5
6	44829b	2.25"	N	Bachmann	4
7	44861	LT	N	Bachmann	1
8	44862	RT	N	Bachmann	5
9	44887	30"	N	Bachmann	11
10	44891	HB	N	Bachmann	4	Bumper
11	44897	10" FD	N	Bachmann	8
12	44899a	1.5"	N	Bachmann	2
13	44899d	0.75"	N	Bachmann	2

Total: 100

37. Bachmann HO Scale EZ Track Nickel Silver 134" x 107"

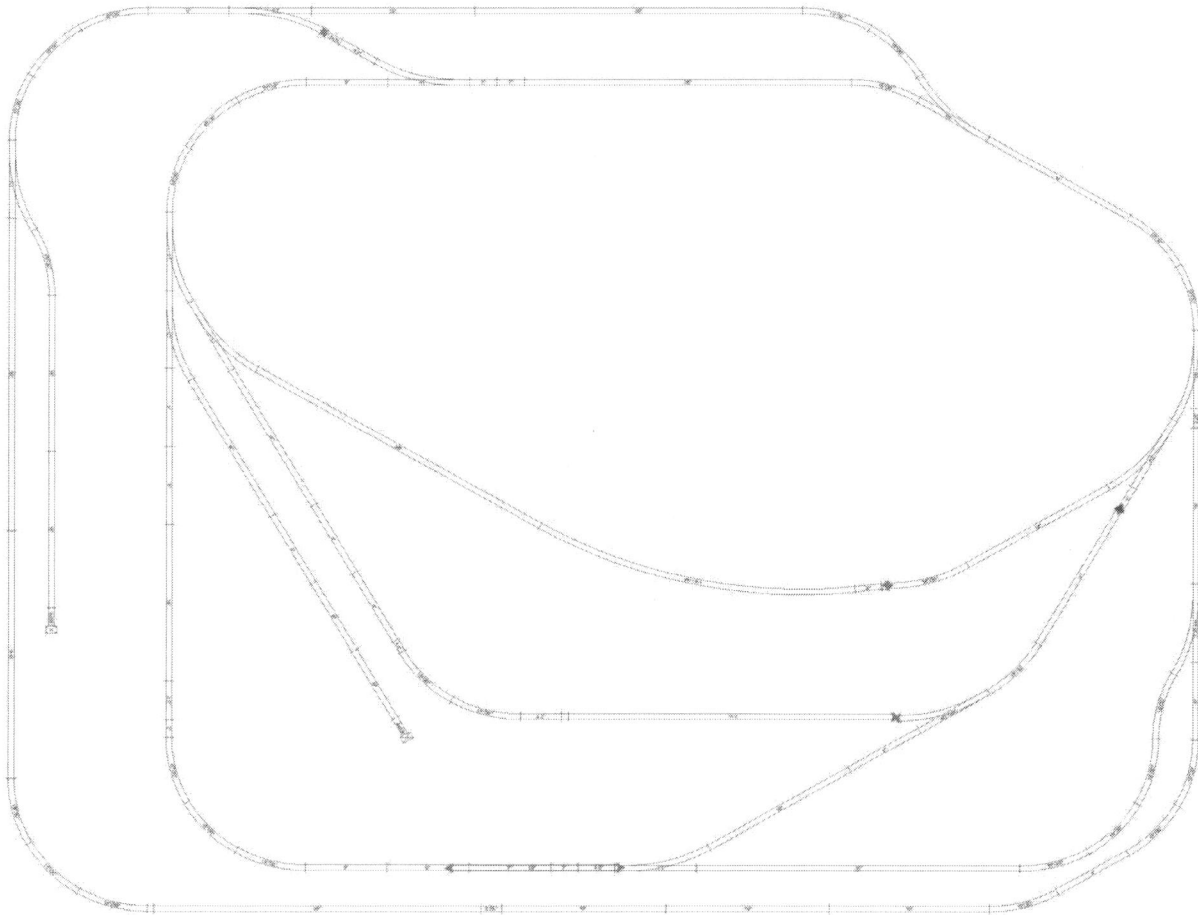

Part #   Type   Brand Qty.

#	Part #	Type	Brand		Qty.	
1	44131	RT DCC HO	Bachmann		2	
2	44371	36" Flex	HO	Bachmann	3	
3	44501	18"/30°	HO	Bachmann	1	
4	44505	15"/30°	HO	Bachmann	28	
5	44511	9"	HO	Bachmann	15	
6	44512	3"	HO	Bachmann	5	
7	44513	2.25"	HO	Bachmann	2	
8	44514	4.5"	HO	Bachmann	4	
9	44541s	2" 541s	HO	Bachmann	1	
10	44561	LT	HO	Bachmann	5	
11	44562	RT	HO	Bachmann	5	
12	44584	36"	HO	Bachmann	6	
13	44588	18"	HO	Bachmann	15	
14	44591	44591	HO	Bachmann	2	Hayes Bumper
15	44592-1	0.75"	HO	Bachmann	3	
16	44592-4	1.5"	HO	Bachmann	1	
17	44592-5	2"	HO	Bachmann	1	

Total: 99

38. Life-Like HO Scale Power-loc Track Nickel Silver 88" x 111"

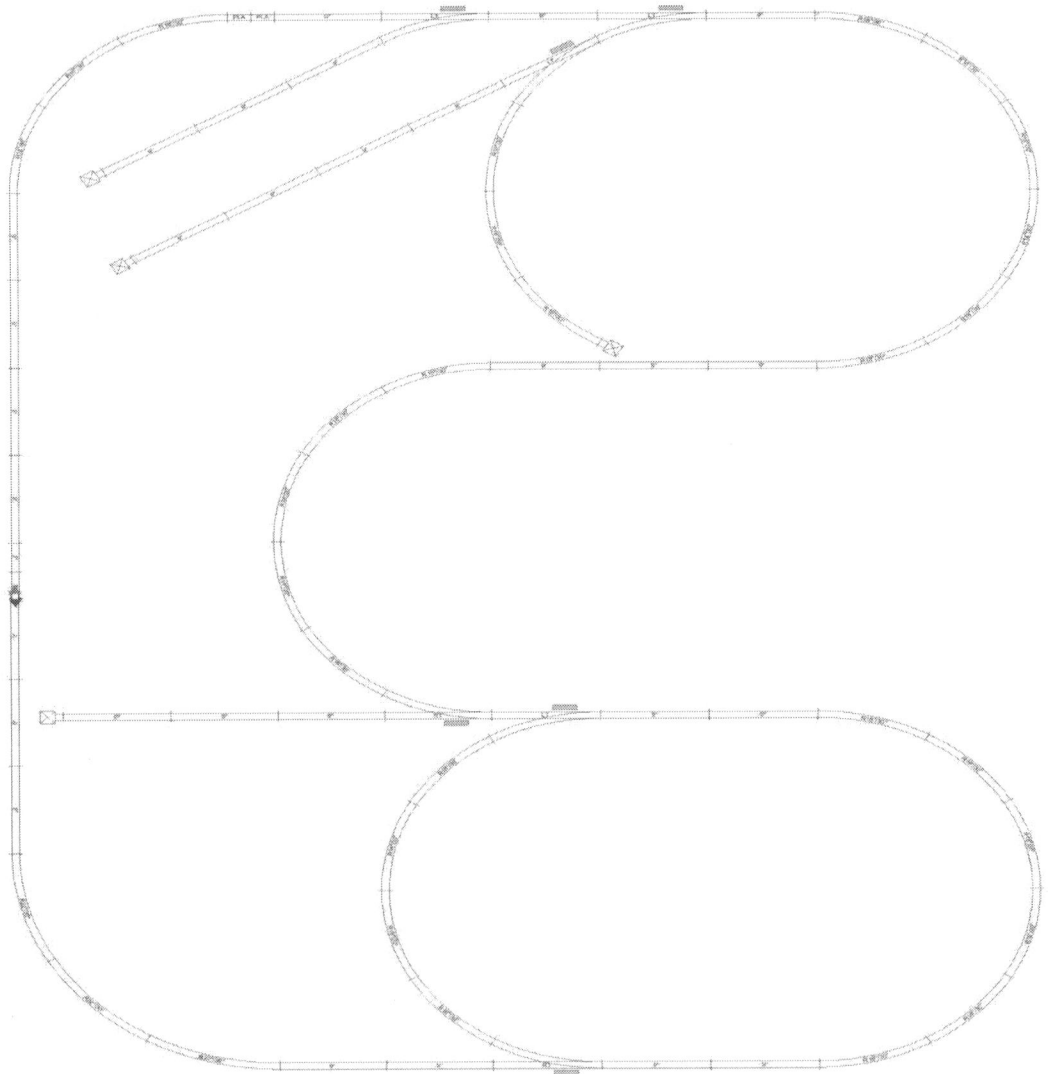

	Part #		Type	Brand	Qty.	
1	21332	9"	HO	Walthers	29	
2	21333	R18"/30°	HO	Walthers	27	
3	21335	LT	HO	Walthers	4	Remote Turnout
4	21336	RT	HO	Walthers	2	Remote Turnout
5	21338	Bmp	HO	Walthers	4	Bumper
6	21344	PLA	HO	Walthers	2	Power-Link Adapter track
7	21347	3"	HO	Walthers	2	
8	21348	R22"/30°	HO	Walthers	3	

Total: 73

39. Life-Like HO Scale Power-loc Track Nickel Silver 96" x 124"

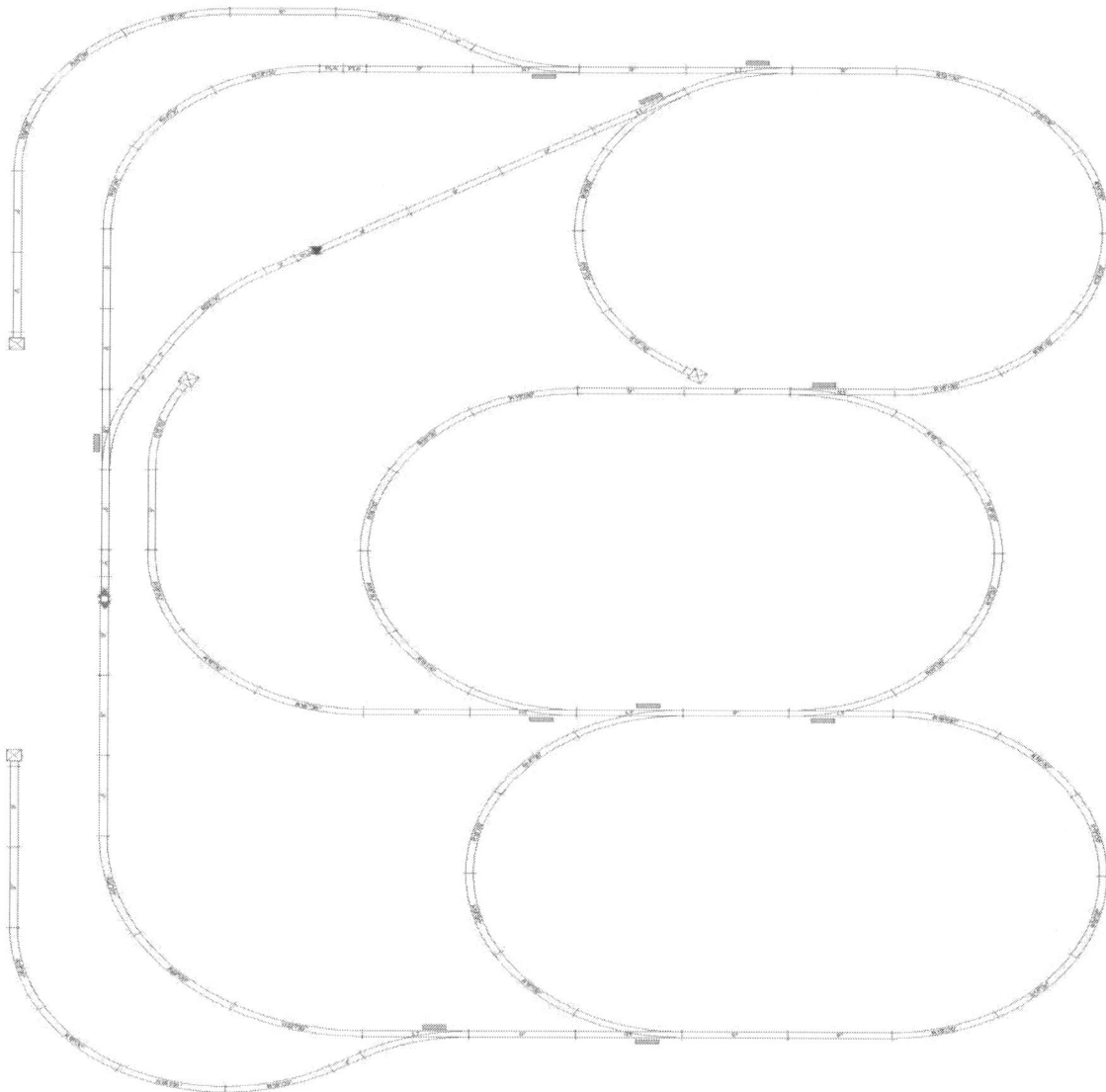

	Part #		Type	Brand	Qty.	
1	21332	9"	HO	Walthers	25	
2	21333	R18"/30°	HO	Walthers	43	
3	21335	LT	HO	Walthers	5	Remote Turnout
4	21336	RT	HO	Walthers	5	Remote Turnout
5	21338	Bmp	HO	Walthers	4	Bumper
6	21344	PLA	HO	Walthers	3	Power-Link Adapter track
7	21347	3"	HO	Walthers	7	
8	21348	R22"/30°	HO	Walthers	4	

Total: 96

40. Life-Like HO Scale Power-loc Track Nickel Silver 143" x 62"

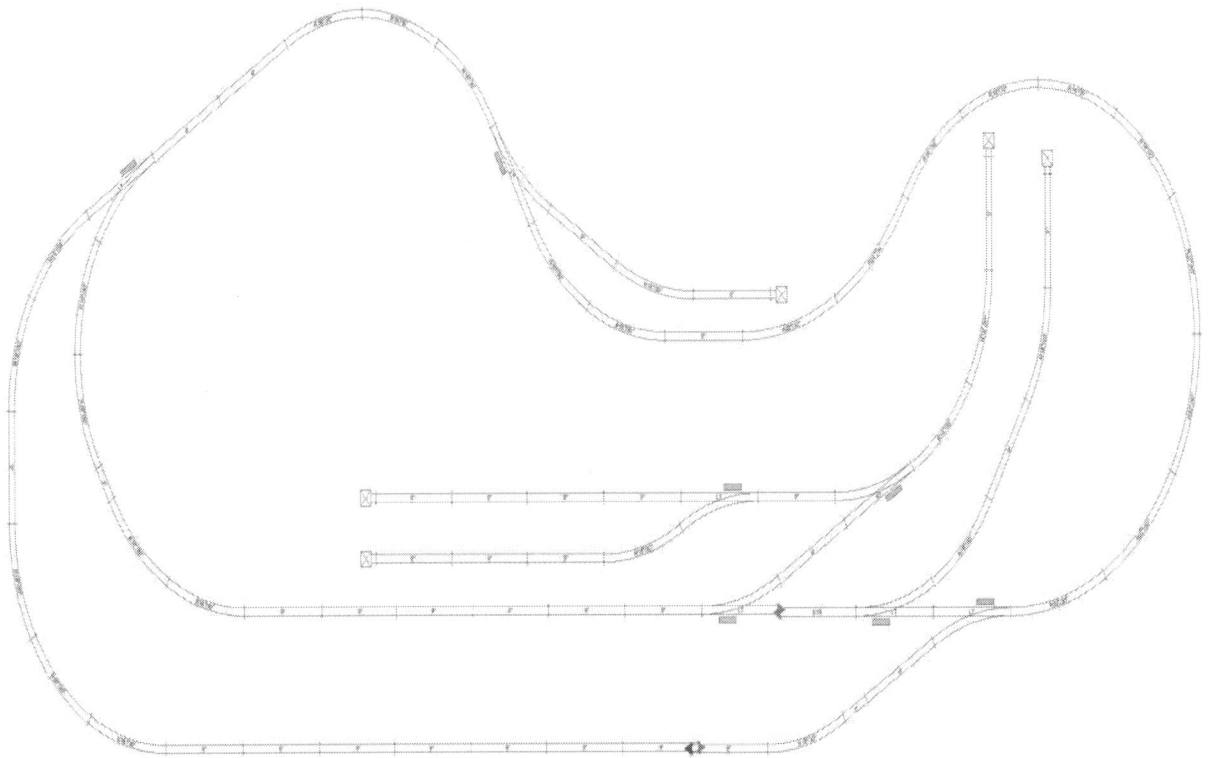

	Part #	Type	Brand	Qty.		
1	21332	9"	HO	Walthers	33	
2	21333	R18"/30°	HO	Walthers	25	
3	21335	LT	HO	Walthers	6	Remote Turnout
4	21336	RT	HO	Walthers	1	Remote Turnout
5	21338	Bmp	HO	Walthers	5	Bumper
6	21347	3"	HO	Walthers	2	
7	21348	R22"/30°	HO	Walthers	6	
8	21394	STR	HO	Walthers	1	Straight Terminal Rerailer

Total: 79

41. Life-Like HO Scale Power-loc Track Nickel Silver 148" x 66"

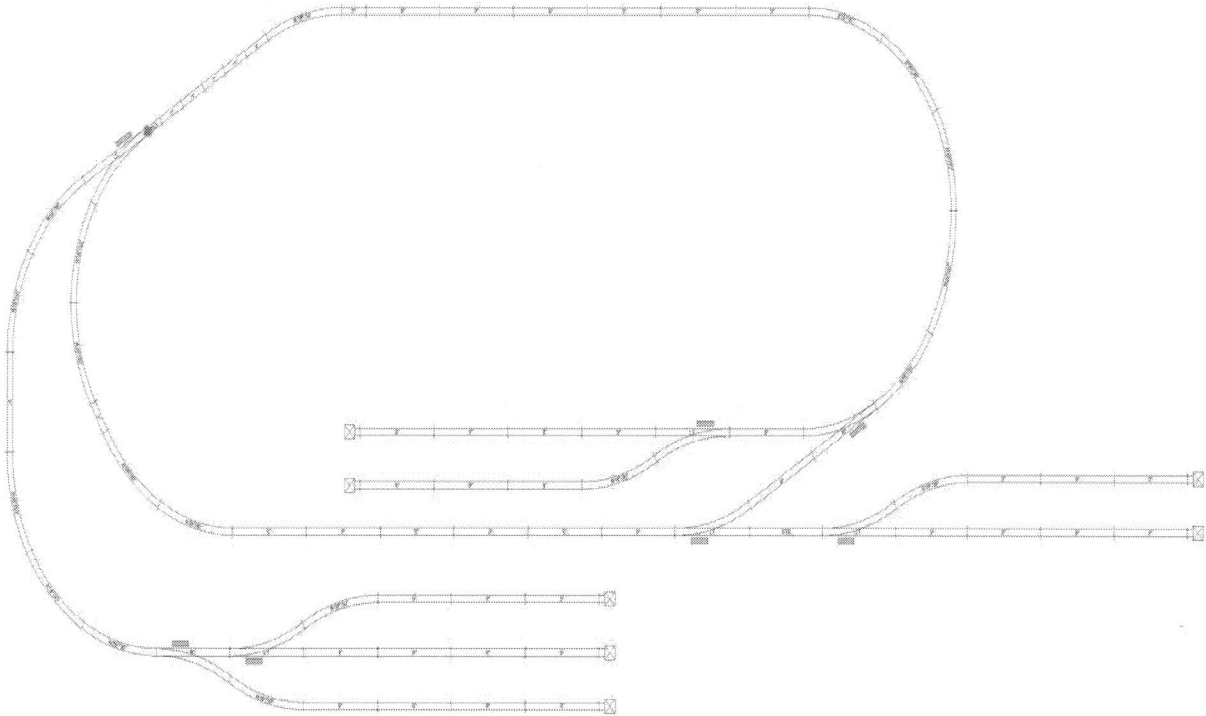

Part #   Type Brand Qty.

#	Part #	Type	Brand		Qty.	Description
1	21332	9"	HO	Walthers	40	
2	21333	R18"/30°	HO	Walthers	18	
3	21335	LT	HO	Walthers	5	Remote Turnout
4	21336	RT	HO	Walthers	2	Remote Turnout
5	21338	Bmp	HO	Walthers	7	Bumper
6	21344	PLA	HO	Walthers	1	Power-Link Adapter track
7	21347	3"	HO	Walthers	7	
8	21348	R22"/30°	HO	Walthers	1	
9	21394	STR	HO	Walthers	1	Straight Terminal Rerailer

Total: 82

42. Atlas HO Scale TR2 Track 126" x 150"

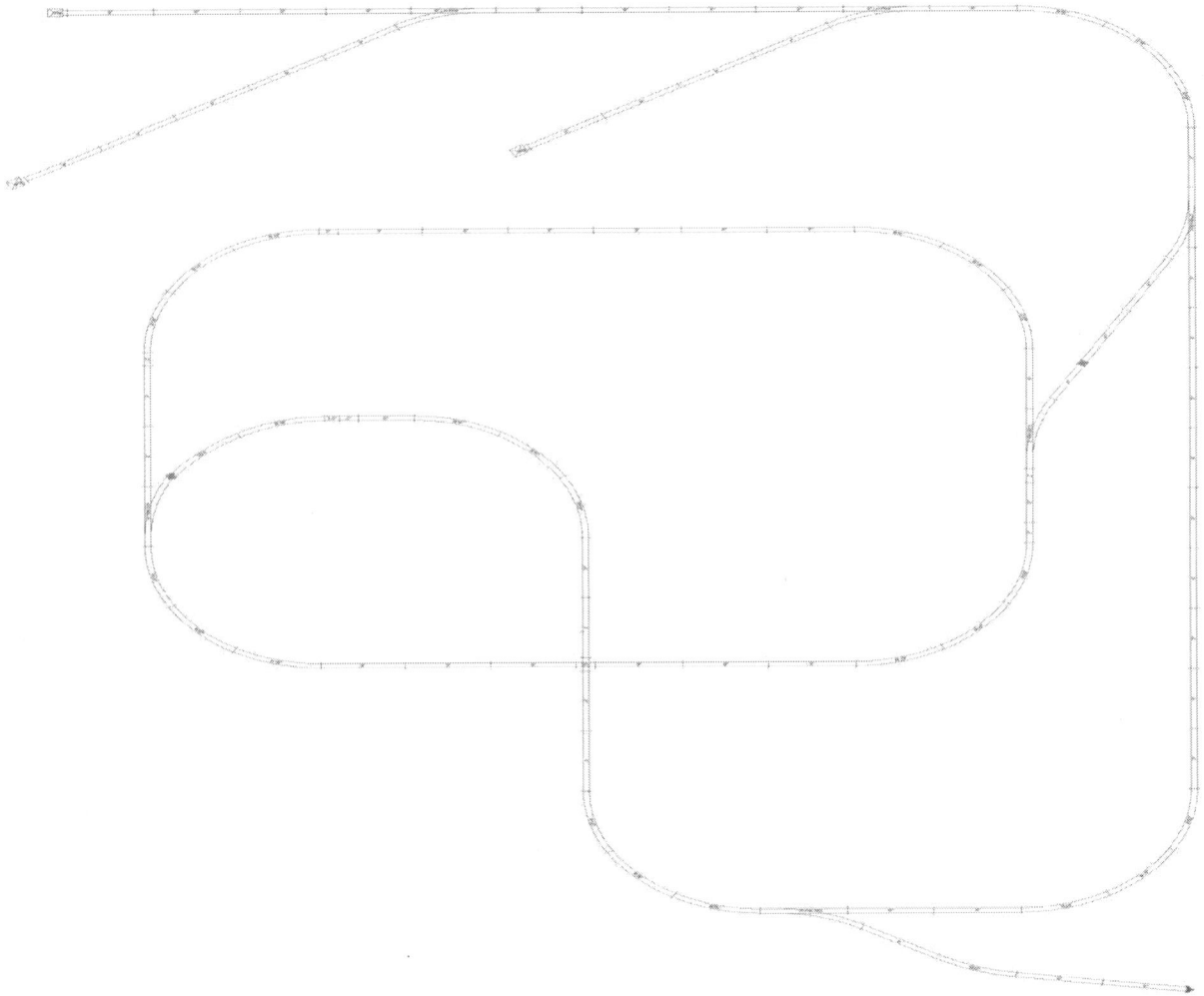

Part #   Type   Brand   Qty.

	Part #	Type	Brand		Qty.		
1	450	9"	HO	Atlas	54		
2	451	6"	HO	Atlas	3		
3	452	3"	HO	Atlas	1		
4	453	1.5"	HO	Atlas	1		
5	454	2"	HO	Atlas	4		
6	460	R18"	HO	Atlas	25		
7	463	R22"	HO	Atlas	1		
8	468	R24"	HO	Atlas	1		
9	470	Bmp	HO	Atlas	3	Bumper	
10	476	90°	HO	Atlas	1		
11	479	9" RH Mnl	HO	Atlas	2	9" Manual Snap Switch	
12	480	9" LH Rmt	HO	Atlas	2	9" Remote Snap Switch	
13	481	9" RH Rmt	HO	Atlas	2	9" Remote Snap Switch	

Total: 100

43. Atlas HO Scale TR2 Track 145" x 113"

	Part #		Type	Brand	Qty.		
1	450	9"	HO	Atlas	37		
2	451	6"	HO	Atlas	5		
3	452	3"	HO	Atlas	1		
4	453	1.5"	HO	Atlas	3		
5	454	2"	HO	Atlas	1		
6	460	R18"	HO	Atlas	26		
7	470	Bmp	HO	Atlas	8	Bumper	
8	478	9" LH Mnl	HO	Atlas	5	9" Manual Snap Switch	
9	479	9" RH Mnl	HO	Atlas	3	9" Manual Snap Switch	
10	480	9" LH Rmt	HO	Atlas	1	9" Remote Snap Switch	
11	481	9" RH Rmt	HO	Atlas	1	9" Remote Snap Switch	
Total:	91						

44. Bachmann HO Scale EZ Track Nickel Silver 123" x 78"

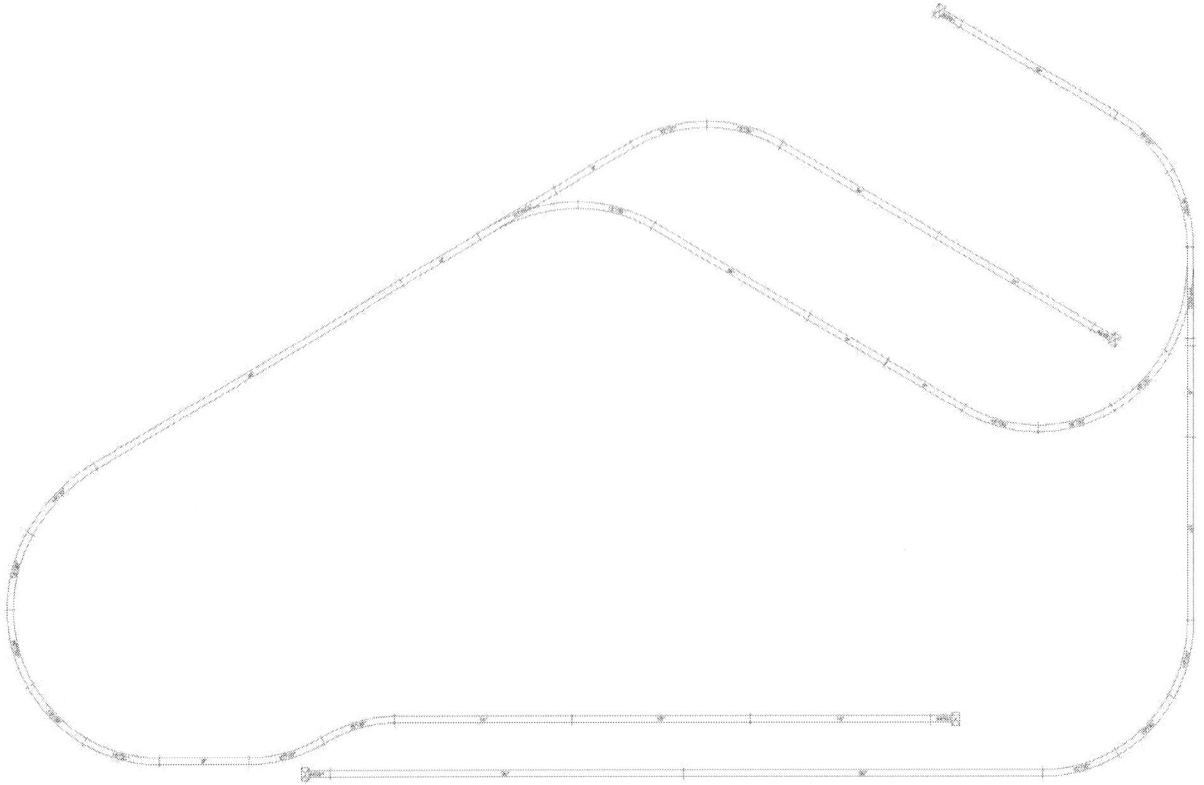

	Part #	Type	Brand	Qty.	
1	44131	RT DCC HO	Bachmann	2	
2	44501	18"/30°	HO Bachmann	1	
3	44505	15"/30°	HO Bachmann	17	
4	44511	9" HO	Bachmann	6	
5	44584	36" HO	Bachmann	3	
6	44588	18" HO	Bachmann	8	
7	44591	44591 HO	Bachmann	4	Hayes Bumper
8	44592-1	0.75" HO	Bachmann	1	

Total: 42

45. Bachmann HO Scale EZ Track Nickel Silver 142" x 95"

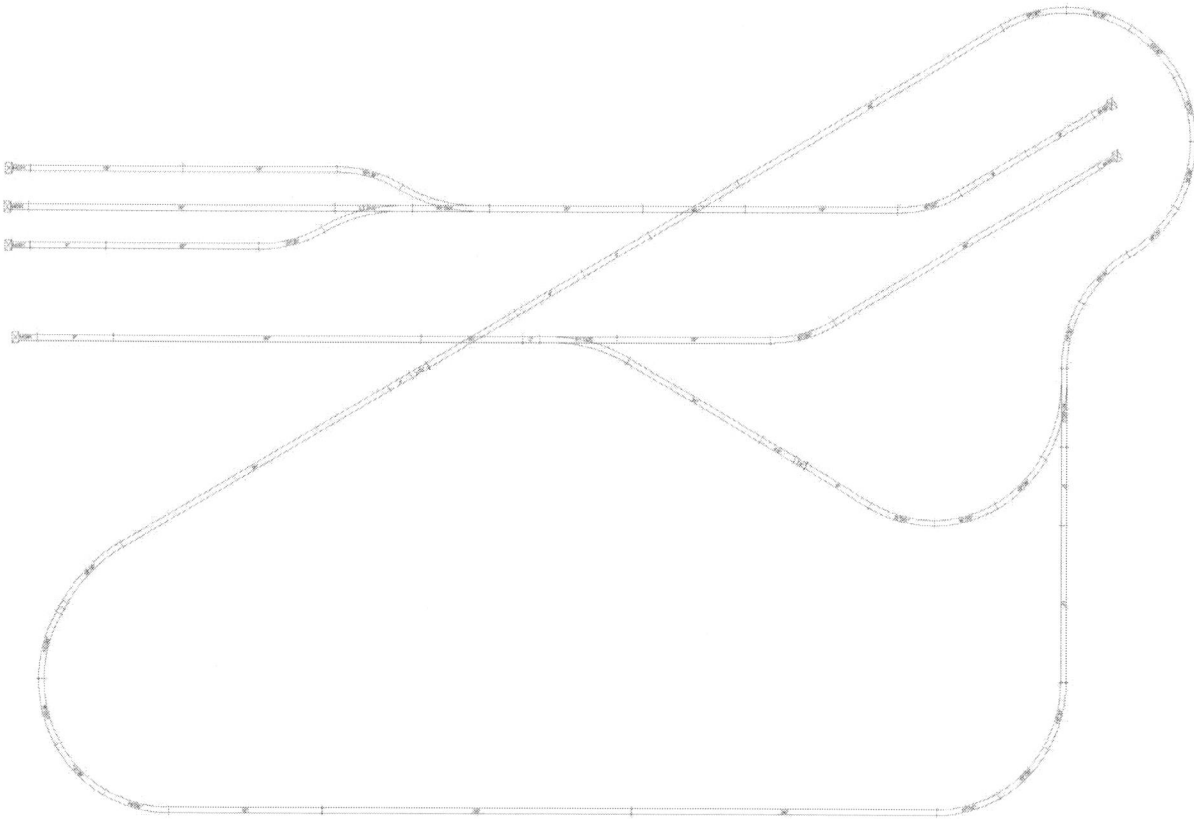

	Part #	Type	Brand	Qty.	
1	44130	LT DCC HO	Bachmann	1	
2	44131	RT DCC HO	Bachmann	3	
3	44501	18"/30°	HO Bachmann	1	
4	44505	15"/30°	HO Bachmann	22	
5	44511	9" HO	Bachmann	8	
6	44512	3" HO	Bachmann	1	
7	44513	2.25" HO	Bachmann	1	
8	44514	4.5" HO	Bachmann	1	
9	44540	30° HO	Bachmann	2	
10	44584	36" HO	Bachmann	7	
11	44588	18" HO	Bachmann	9	
12	44591	44591 HO	Bachmann	6	Hayes Bumper
13	44592-1	0.75"	HO Bachmann	2	
14	44592-4	1.5"	HO Bachmann	1	
15	44592-5	2"	HO Bachmann	1	

Total: 66

46. Bachmann HO Scale EZ Track Nickel Silver 167" x 117"

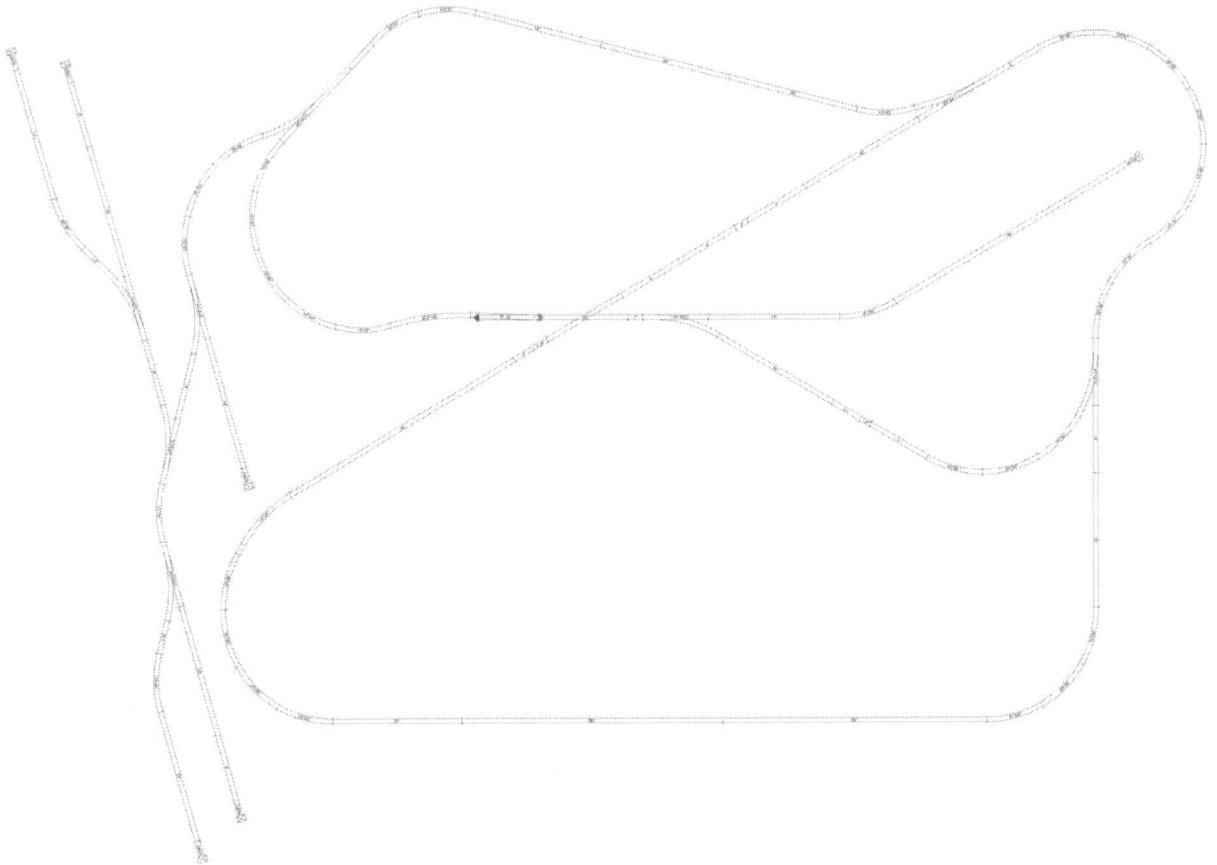

Part #   Type   Brand Qty.

	Part #	Type		Brand	Qty.	
1	44130	LT DCC	HO	Bachmann	2	
2	44131	RT DCC	HO	Bachmann	5	
3	44501	18"/30°	HO	Bachmann	1	
4	44505	15"/30°	HO	Bachmann	33	
5	44507	35.5"/18°	HO	Bachmann	1	
6	44511	9"	HO	Bachmann	13	
7	44512	3"	HO	Bachmann	1	
8	44513	2.25"	HO	Bachmann	1	
9	44514	4.5"	HO	Bachmann	3	
10	44540	30°	HO	Bachmann	1	
11	44558	RT #4	HO	Bachmann	1	
12	44584	36"	HO	Bachmann	4	
13	44588	18"	HO	Bachmann	13	
14	44591	44591	HO	Bachmann	6	Hayes Bumper
15	44592-1	0.75"	HO	Bachmann	3	
16	44592-4	1.5"	HO	Bachmann	1	
17	44592-5	2"	HO	Bachmann	2	

Total: 91

47. Kato HO Scale Uni-Track 215" x 49"

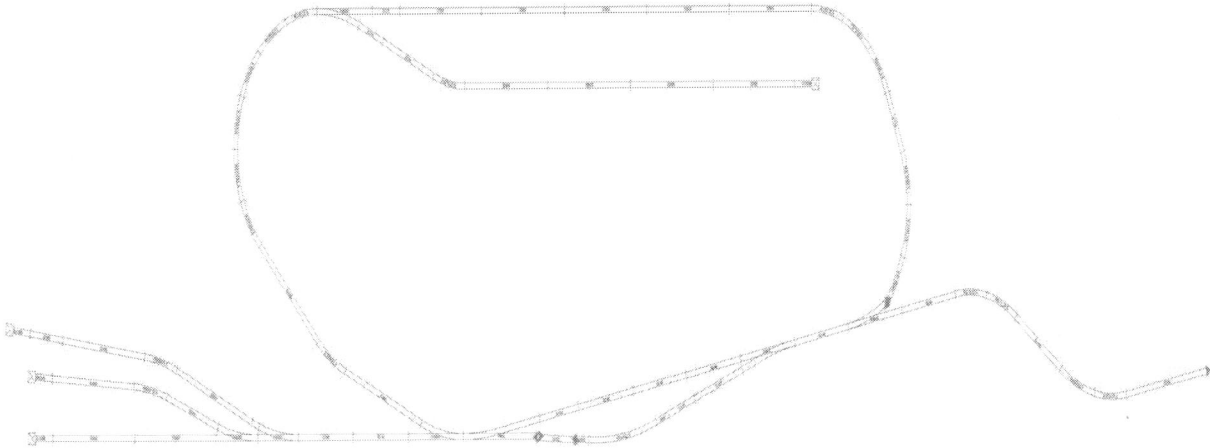

	Part #		Type	Brand	Qty.			
1	2-105	S60	HO	Kato	2			
2	2-120	S114	HO	Kato	1			
3	2-130	S174	HO	Kato	3			
4	2-140	S123	HO	Kato	2			
5	2-150	S246	HO	Kato	10			
6	2-160	S227	HO	Kato	1			
7	2-170	S109B	HO	Kato	4	Track End		
8	2-180	S369	HO	Kato	17			
9	2-193	S149	HO	Kato	1			
10	2-250	R790/22,5		HO	Kato	1		
11	2-260	R430/22,5		HO	Kato	1		
12	2-280	R370/22,5		HO	Kato	16		
13	2-840	P490L	HO	Kato	1			
14	2-841	P490R	HO	Kato	2			
15	2-851	P550R	HO	Kato	2			
16	2-860	P867L	HO	Kato	1			
17	2-862	P#6L	HO	Kato	1			
18	550-15,5		R550/15,5		HO	Kato	3	
19	550-3,5	R550/3,5		HO	Kato	1		

Total: 70

48. Kato HO Scale Uni-Track 52" x 161"

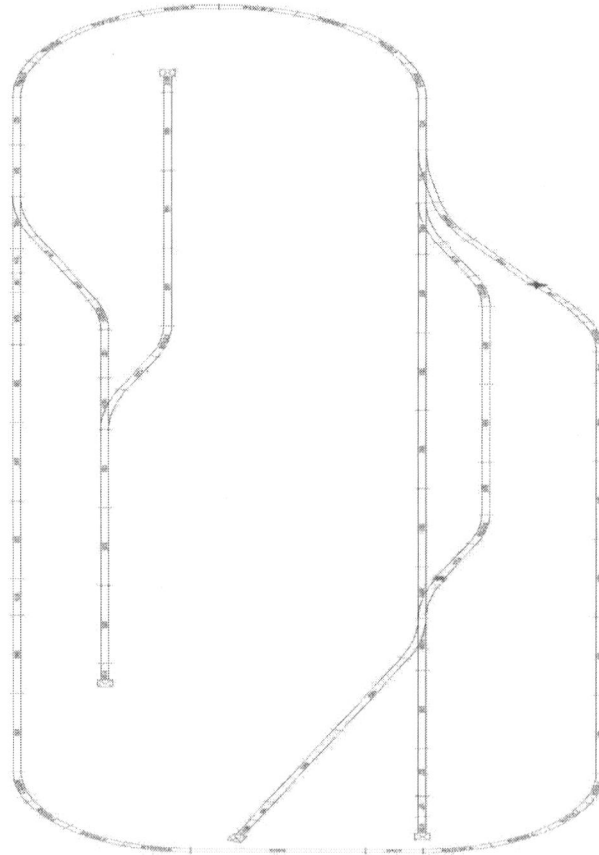

Part #   Type   Brand Qty.

#	Part #	Type	Brand		Qty.	
1	2-111	S94	HO	Kato	2	
2	2-120	S114	HO	Kato	1	
3	2-130	S174	HO	Kato	5	
4	2-140	S123	HO	Kato	1	
5	2-150	S246	HO	Kato	5	
6	2-160	S227	HO	Kato	3	
7	2-170	S109B	HO	Kato	4	Track End
8	2-180	S369	HO	Kato	26	
9	2-193	S149	HO	Kato	2	
10	2-260	R430/22,5	HO	Kato	8	
11	2-270	R490/22,5	HO	Kato	1	
12	2-280	R370/22,5	HO	Kato	13	
13	2-840	P490L	HO	Kato	2	
14	2-841	P490R	HO	Kato	3	
15	2-860	P867L	HO	Kato	1	
16	550-3,5	R550/3,5	HO	Kato	3	
17	97	S97	HO	Kato	2	

Total: 82

49. Kato HO Scale Uni-Track 61" x 144"

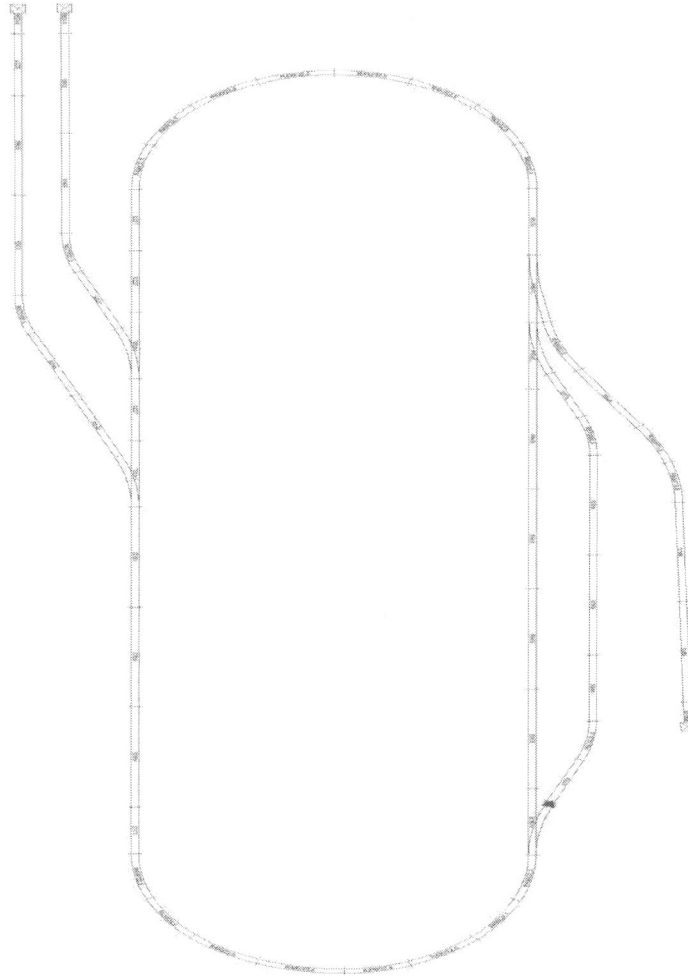

	Part #		Type	Brand	Qty.	
1	2-130	S174	HO	Kato	3	
2	2-150	S246	HO	Kato	5	
3	2-160	S227	HO	Kato	5	
4	2-170	S109B	HO	Kato	3	Track End
5	2-180	S369	HO	Kato	15	
6	2-260	R430/22,5	HO	Kato	14	
7	2-270	R490/22,5	HO	Kato	2	
8	2-280	R370/22,5	HO	Kato	5	
9	2-840	P490L	HO	Kato	3	
10	2-841	P490R	HO	Kato	1	
11	2-860	P867L	HO	Kato	1	
12	550-15,5	R550/15,5	HO	Kato	2	

Total: 59

50. Kato HO Scale Uni-Track 120" x 65"

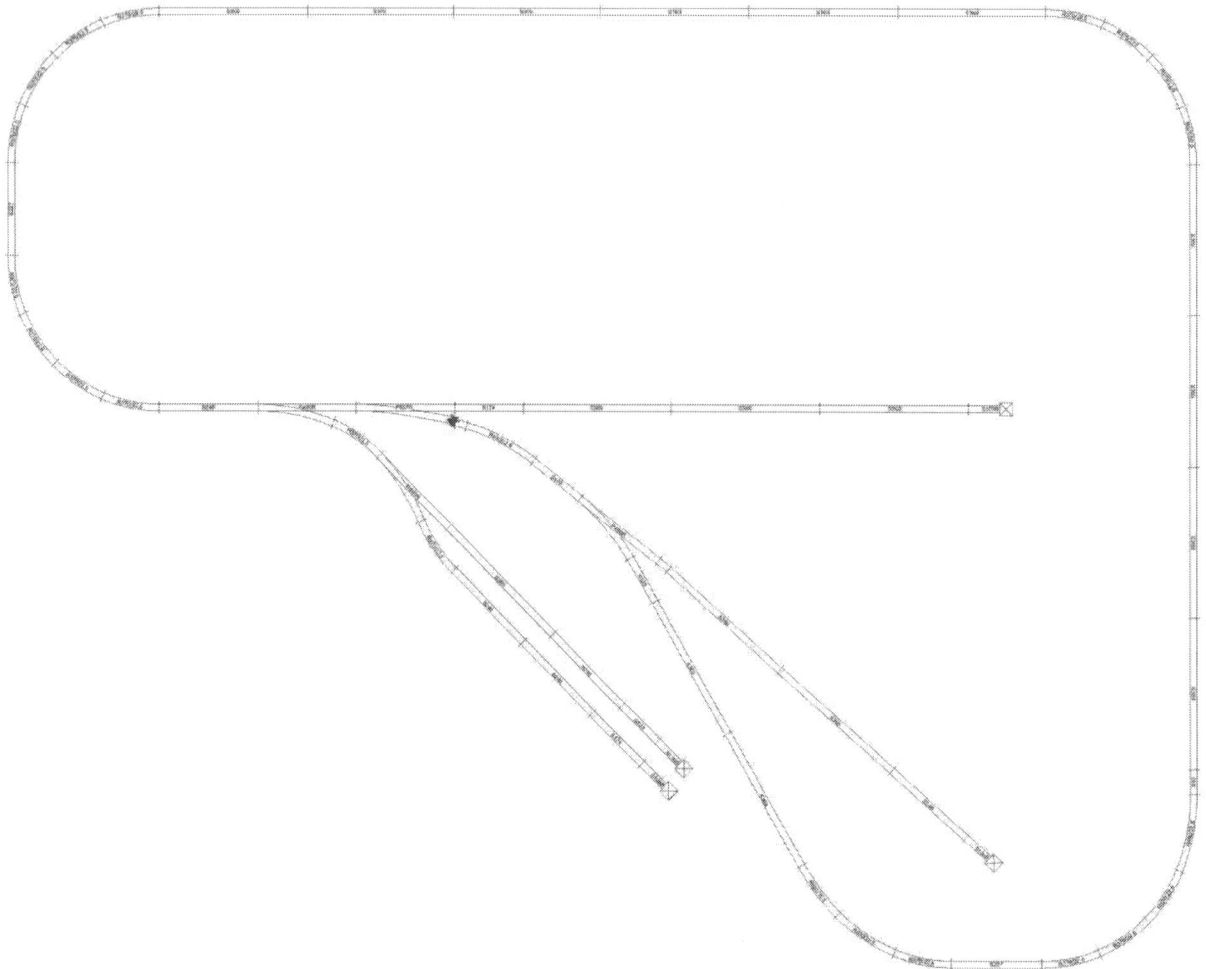

Part #   Type   Brand Qty.

	Part #	Type	Brand	Qty.	
1	2-105	S60	HO	Kato	1
2	2-130	S174	HO	Kato	2
3	2-140	S123	HO	Kato	2
4	2-150	S246	HO	Kato	5
5	2-160	S227	HO	Kato	2
6	2-170	S109B	HO	Kato	4 Track End
7	2-180	S369	HO	Kato	18
8	2-193	S149	HO	Kato	1
9	2-260	R430/22,5	HO	Kato	1
10	2-270	R490/22,5	HO	Kato	2
11	2-280	R370/22,5	HO	Kato	18
12	2-841	P490R	HO	Kato	3
13	2-861	P867R	HO	Kato	1
14	550-15,5	R550/15,5	HO	Kato	1
15	550-3,5	R550/3,5	HO	Kato	2
Total:	63				

51. Kato HO Scale Uni-Track 166" x 92"

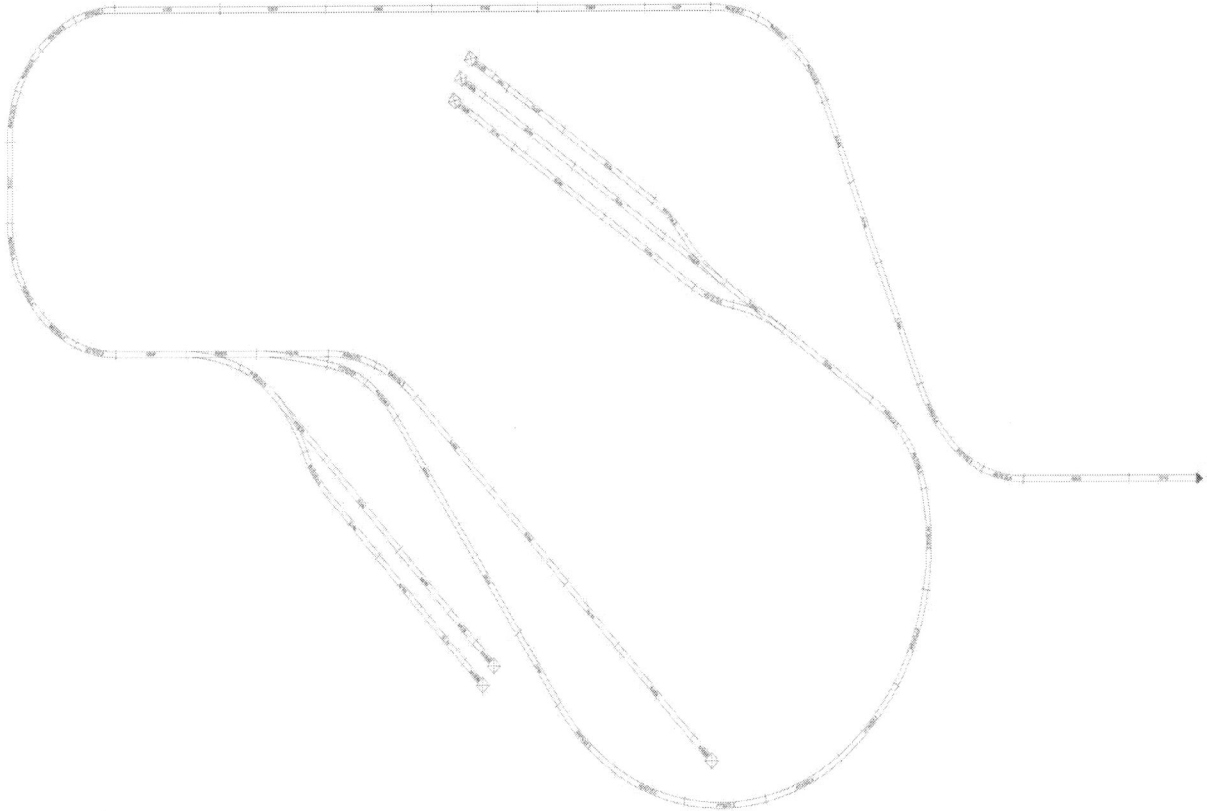

	Part #	Type		Brand	Qty.	
1	2-105	S60	HO	Kato	1	
2	2-130	S174	HO	Kato	1	
3	2-140	S123	HO	Kato	1	
4	2-150	S246	HO	Kato	9	
5	2-160	S227	HO	Kato	3	
6	2-170	S109B	HO	Kato	6	Track End
7	2-180	S369	HO	Kato	19	
8	2-193	S149	HO	Kato	1	
9	2-230	R670/22,5	HO	Kato	2	
10	2-240	R730/22,5	HO	Kato	5	
11	2-260	R430/22,5	HO	Kato	6	
12	2-270	R490/22,5	HO	Kato	1	
13	2-280	R370/22,5	HO	Kato	17	
14	2-840	P490L	HO	Kato	1	
15	2-841	P490R	HO	Kato	3	
16	2-861	P867R	HO	Kato	1	

Total: 77

52. O SCALE LIONEL O TRACK 197" X 129"

53. O SCALE LIONEL O TRACK 135" X 112"

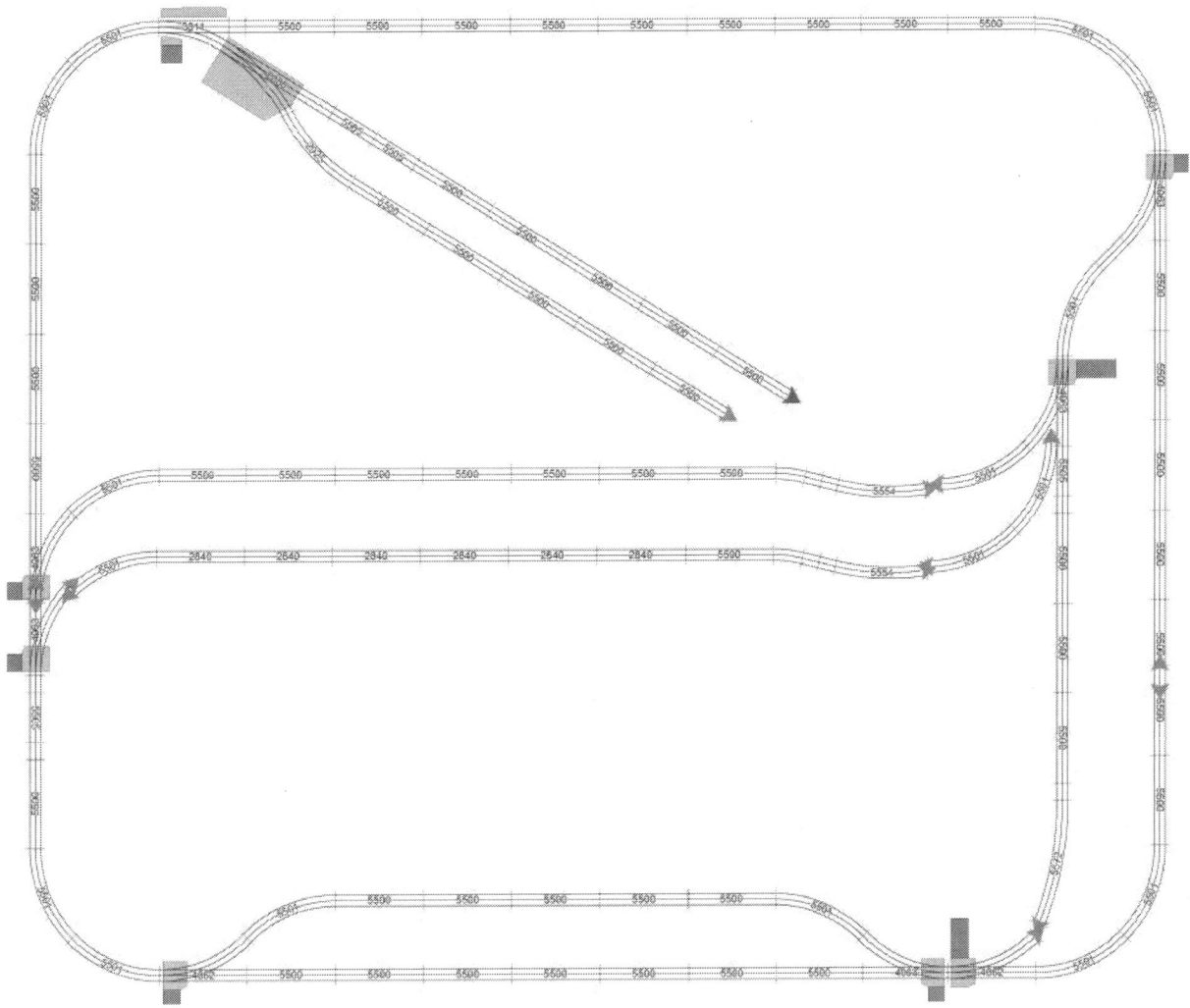

54. O SCALE LIONEL O TRACK 141" X 123"

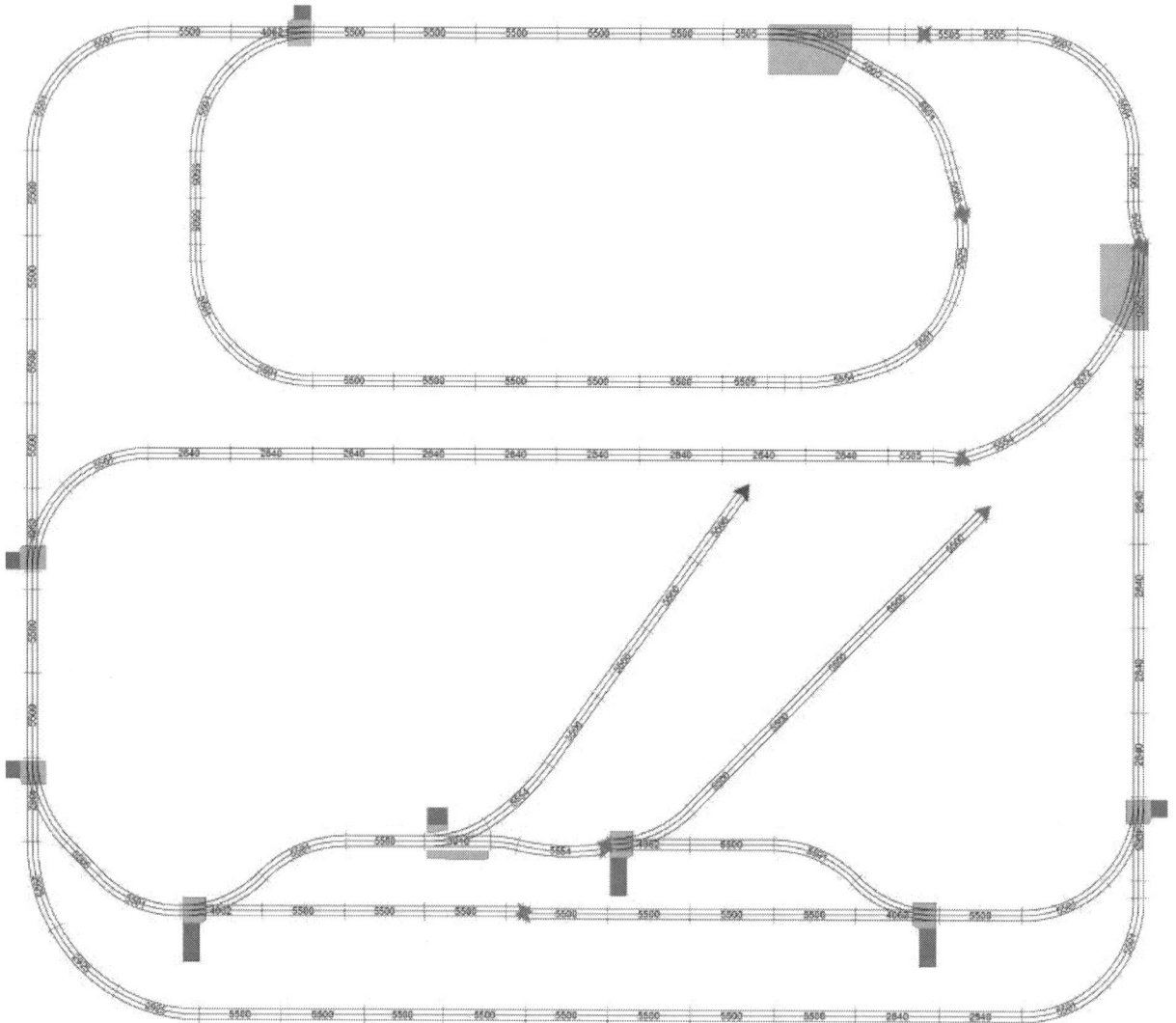

55.   O SCALE LIONEL O TRACK 143" X 142"

56.   O SCALE LIONEL O TRACK 151" X 112"

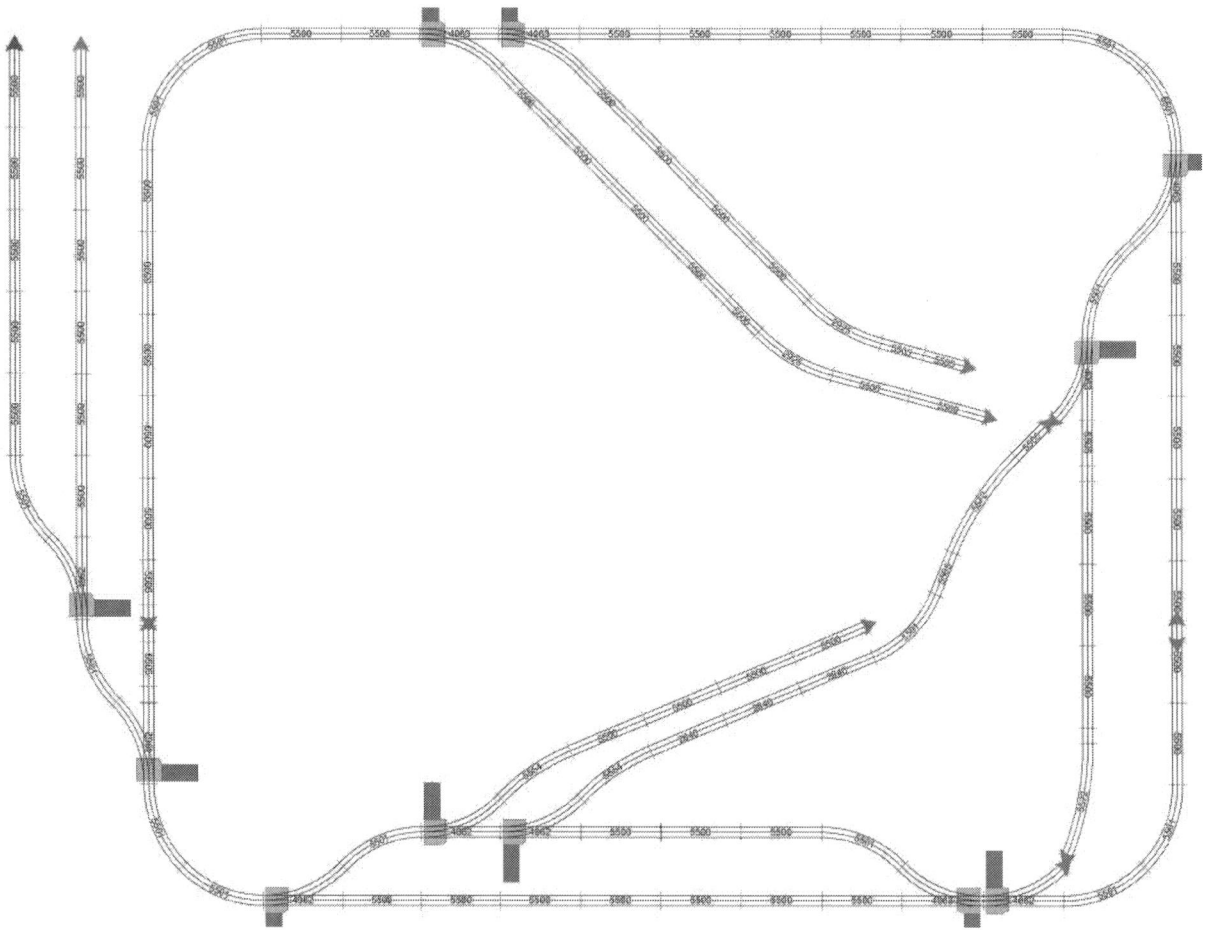

57. O SCALE LIONEL O TRACK 179" X 155"

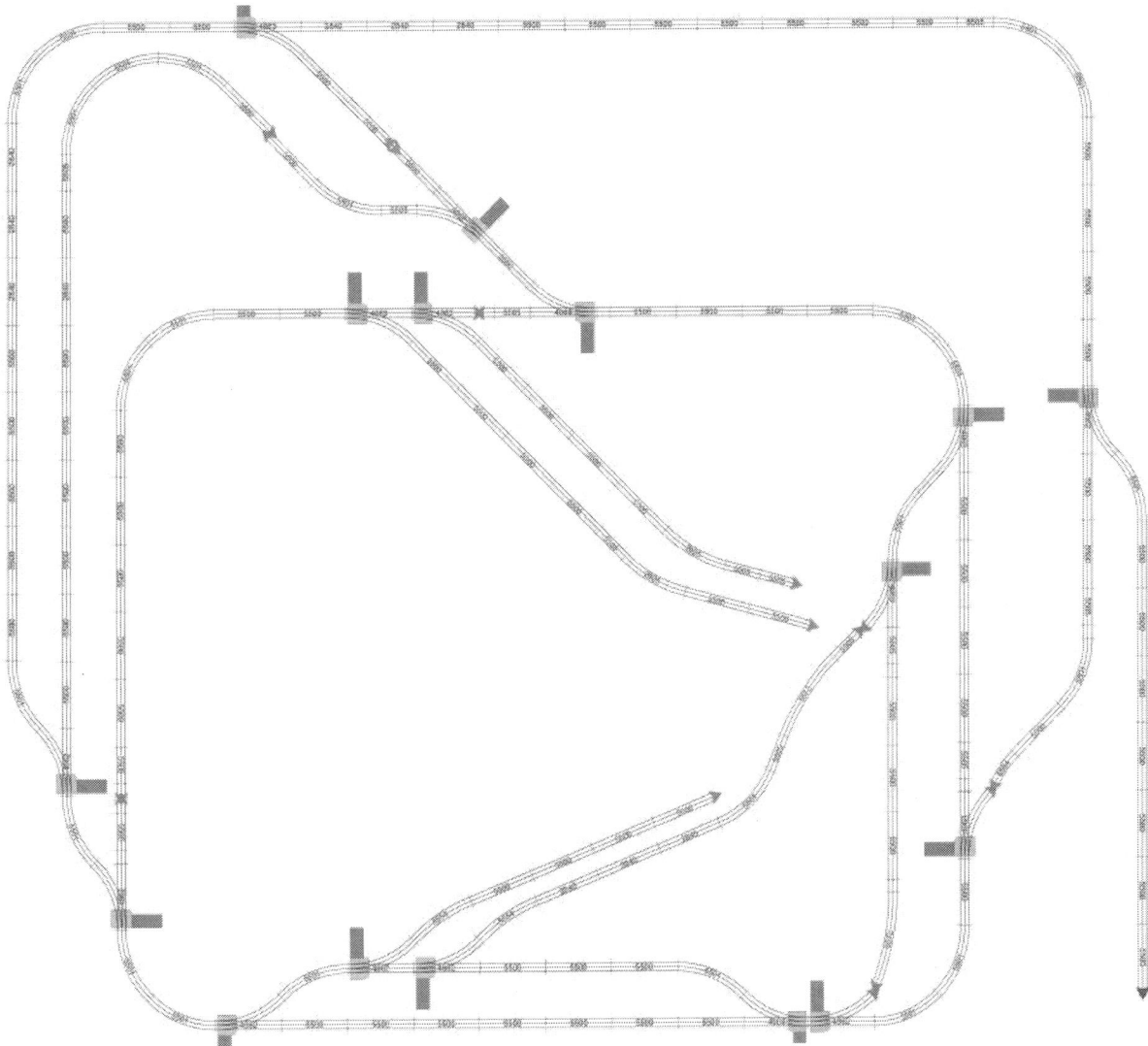

58. O SCALE MTH REAL TRAX 56" X 256"

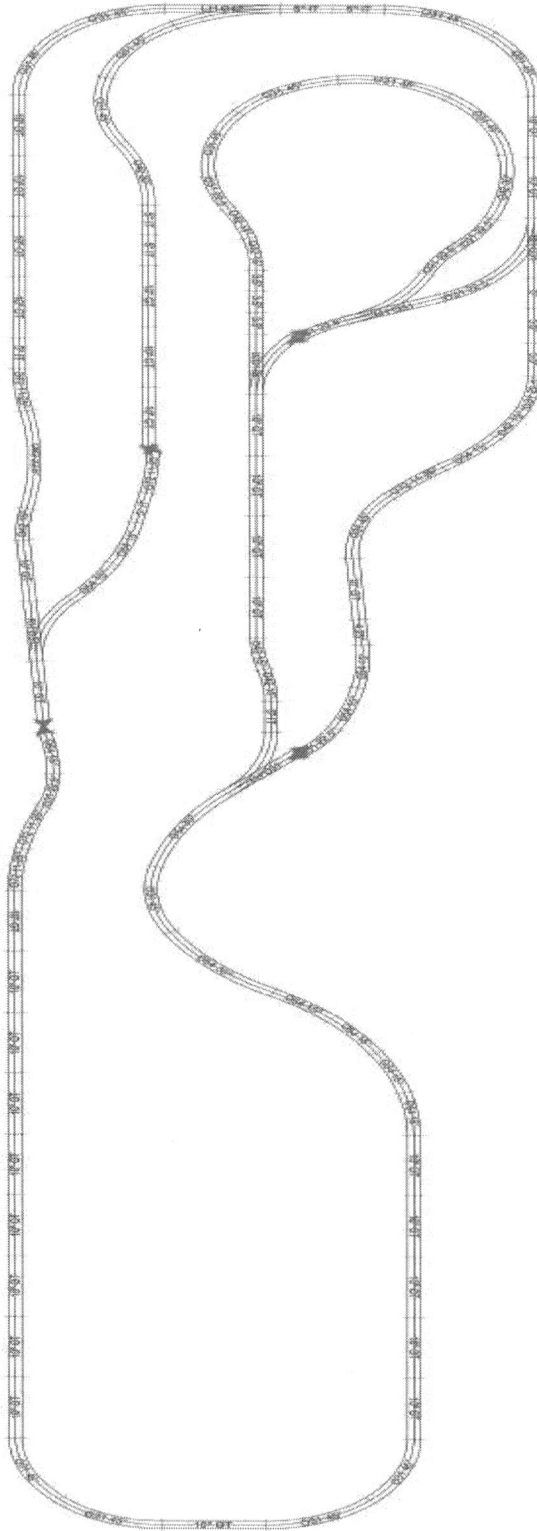

59. O SCALE MTH REAL TRAX 76" X 131"

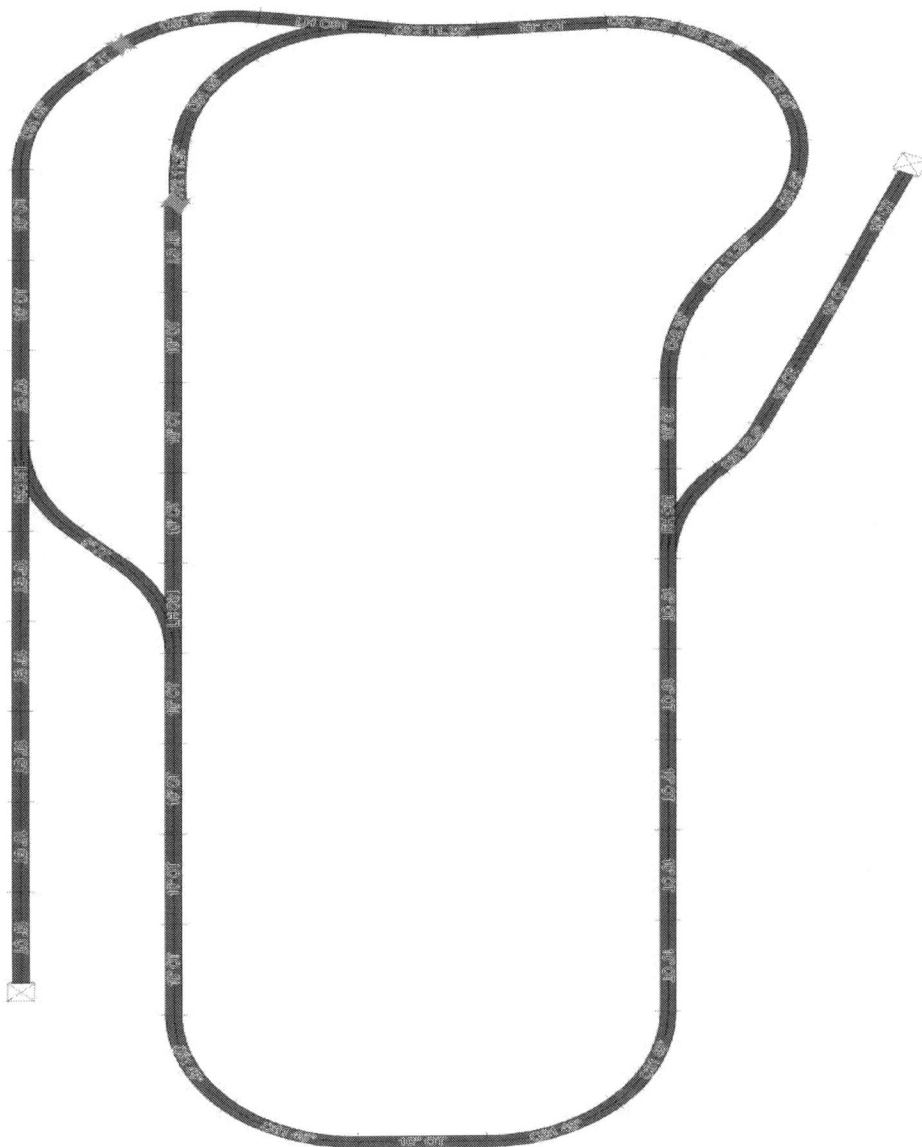

60. O SCALE MTH REAL TRAX 117" X 79"

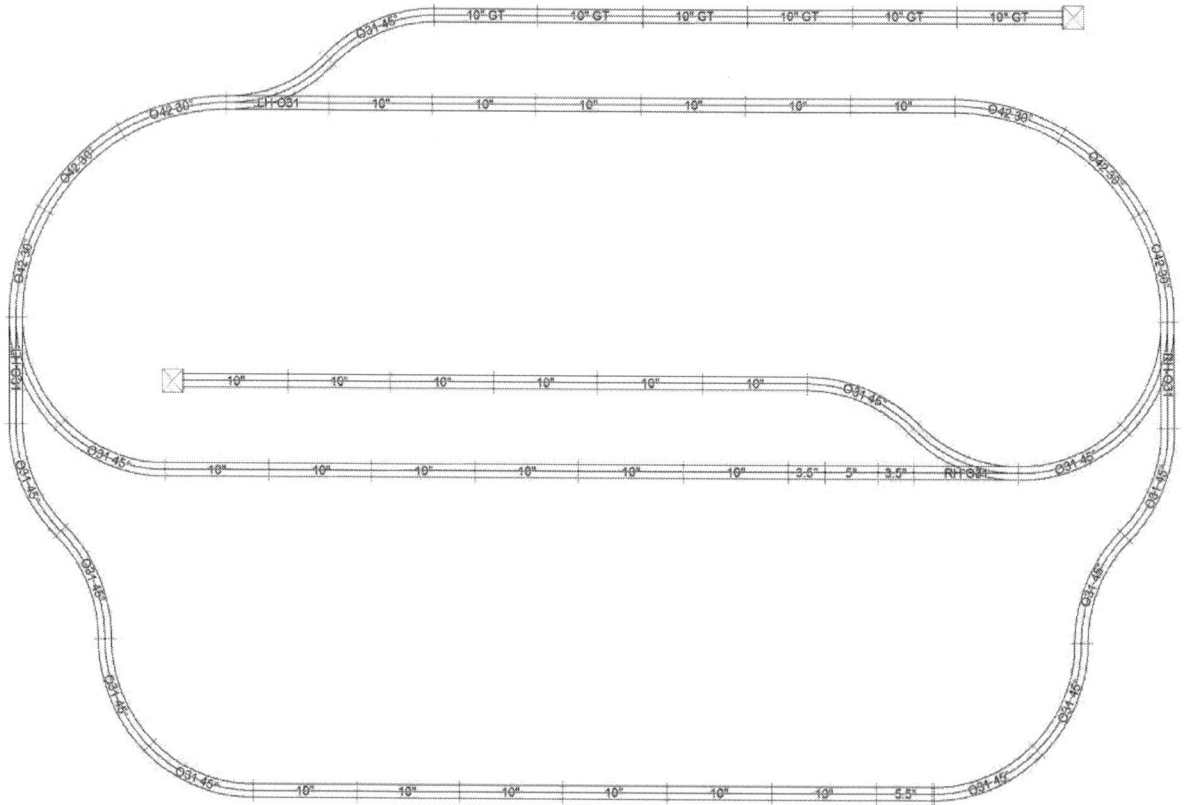

61. O SCALE MTH REAL TRAX 118" X 95"

62. O SCALE MTH REAL TRAX 156" X 152"

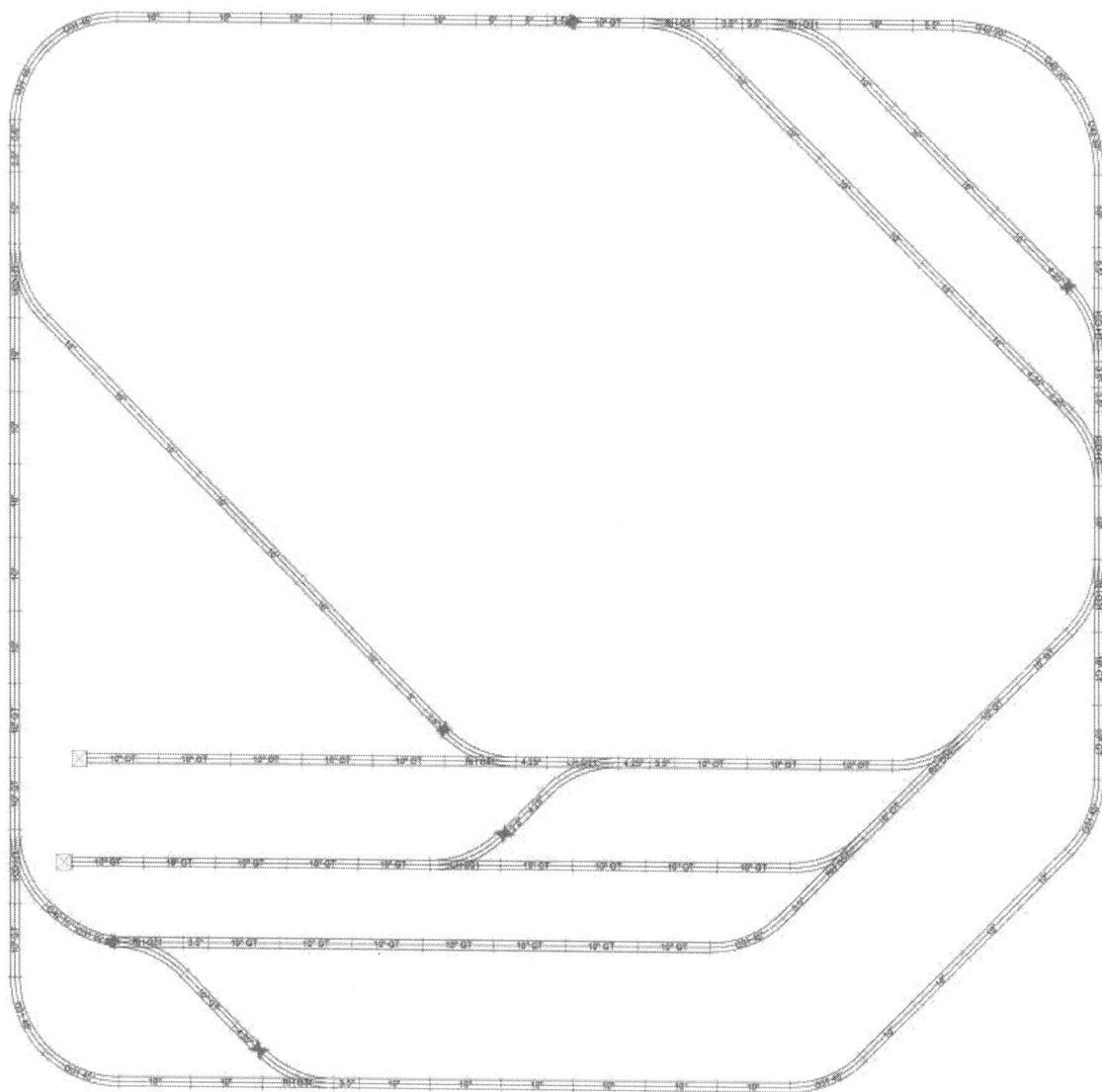

63.   O SCALE MTH REAL TRAX 188" X 148"

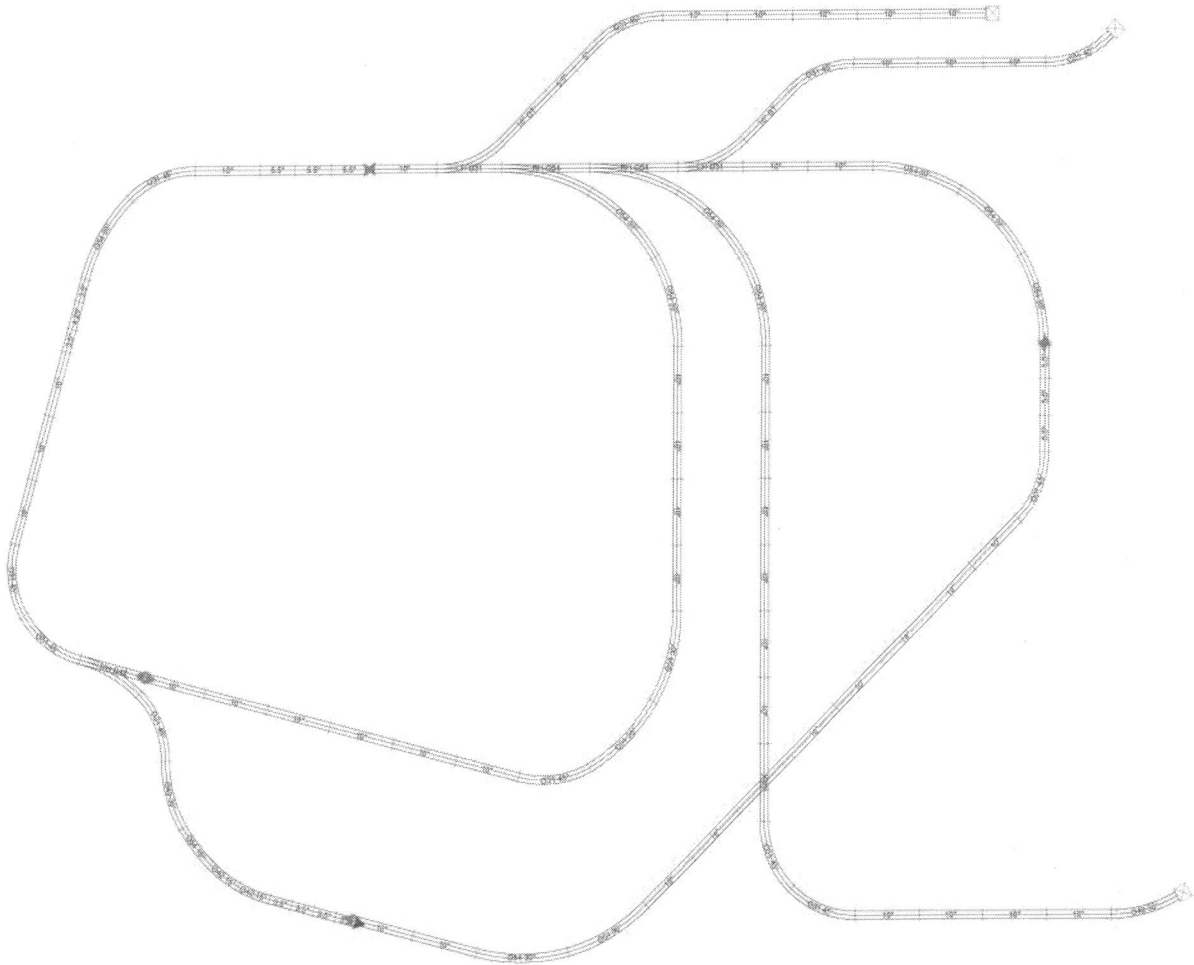

64. Lionel 027 O Scale Track 121" x 109"

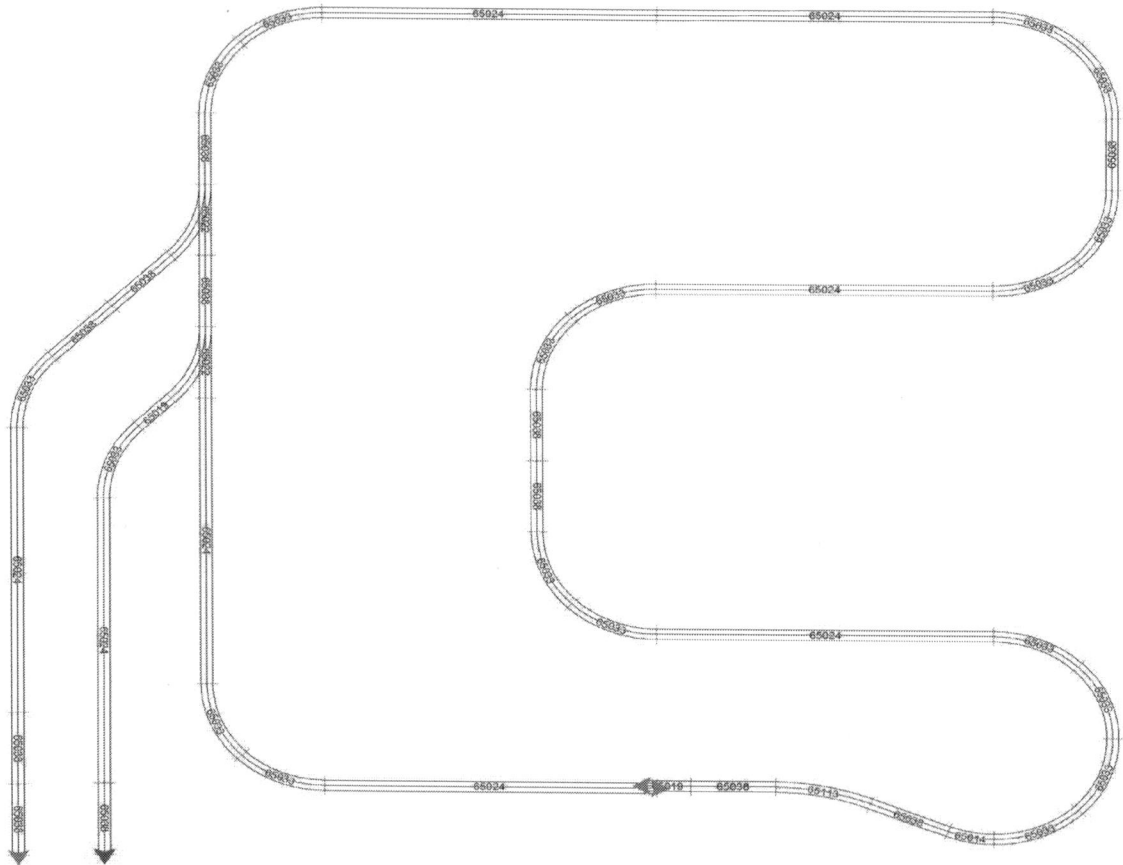

	Part #	Type		Brand	Qty.
1	6-65014	65014	O27	Lionel	1
2	6-65019	65019	O27	Lionel	2
3	6-65022	65022	O27	Lionel	2
4	6-65024	65024	O27	Lionel	8
5	6-65033	65033	O27	Lionel	18
6	6-65038	65038	O27	Lionel	12
7	6-65113	65113	O27	Lionel	1

Total: 44

65. Lionel 027 O Scale Track 154" x 122"

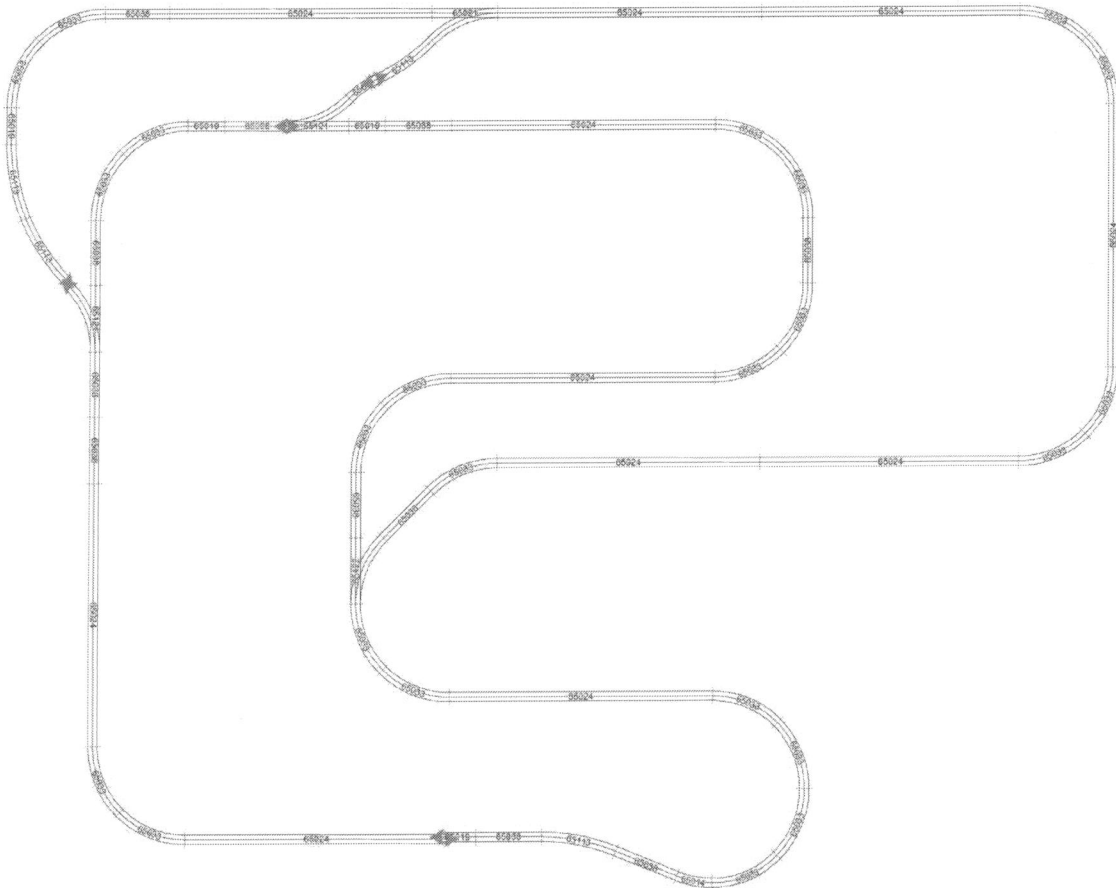

	Part #	Type		Brand	Qty.
1	6-65014	65014	O27	Lionel	2
2	6-65019	65019	O27	Lionel	4
3	6-65021	65021	O27	Lionel	1
4	6-65024	65024	O27	Lionel	11
5	6-65033	65033	O27	Lionel	23
6	6-65038	65038	O27	Lionel	11
7	6-65113	65113	O27	Lionel	4
8	6-65121	65121	O27	Lionel	2
9	6-65122	65122	O27	Lionel	1

Total: 59

66. MTH Real Trax O Scale Track 117" x 125"

Part #		Type	Brand	Qty.	
1	40-1001	10" O	MTH	10	
2	40-1002	O31 45°	O MTH	14	
3	40-1004	RH O31 O	MTH	2	
4	40-1005	LH O31 O	MTH	4	
5	40-1012	5.5" O	MTH	5	
6	40-1017	4.25" O	MTH	3	
7	40-1019	30" O	MTH	10	
8	40-1024	Bmp O	MTH	2	Lighted bumper
Total:	50				

67. MTH Real Trax O Scale Track 129" x 139"

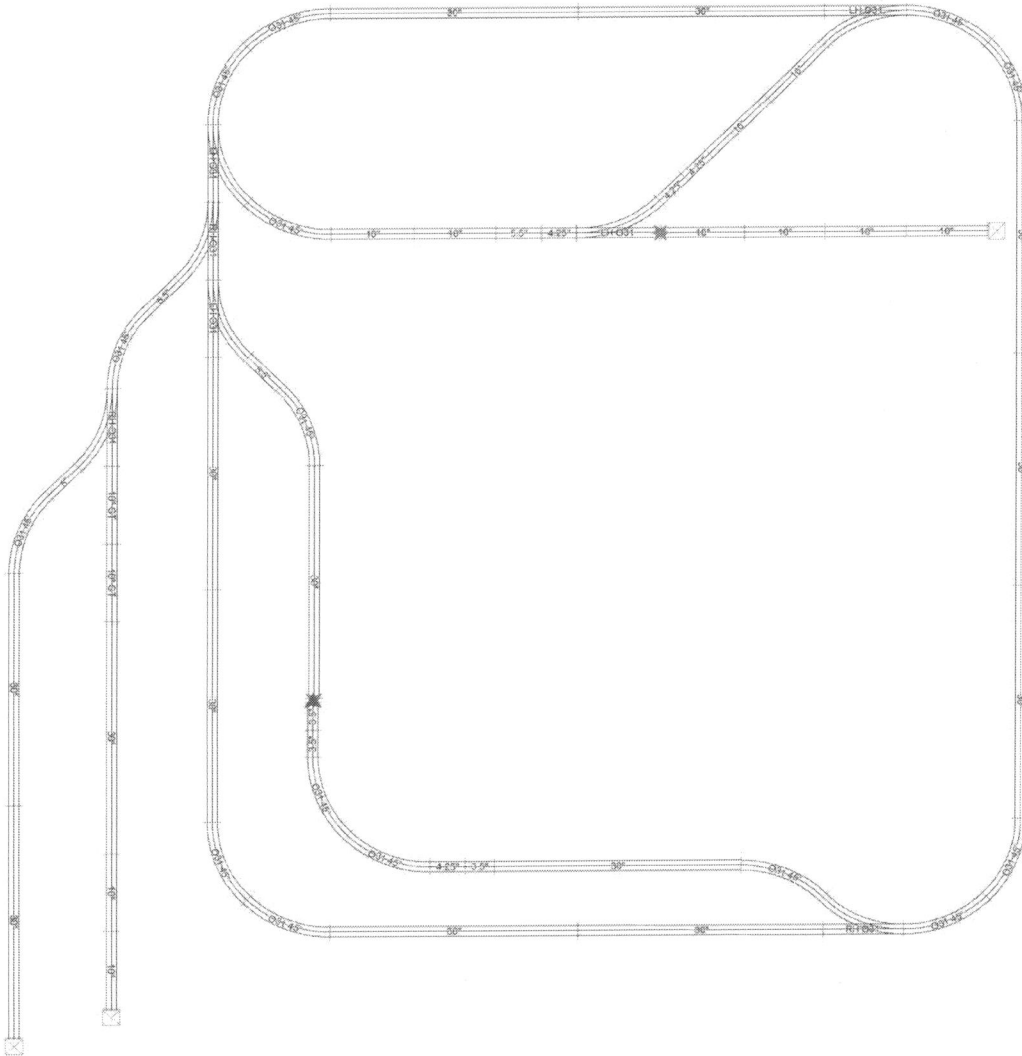

	Part #	Type		Brand	Qty.	
1	40-1001	10"	O	MTH	10	
2	40-1002	O31 45°	O	MTH	15	
3	40-1004	RH O31	O	MTH	3	
4	40-1005	LH O31	O	MTH	4	
5	40-1012	5.5"	O	MTH	3	
6	40-1016	5"	O	MTH	1	
7	40-1017	4.25"	O	MTH	4	
8	40-1018	3.5"	O	MTH	3	
9	40-1019	30"	O	MTH	14	
10	40-1024	Bmp	O	MTH	3	Lighted bumper
11	40-1068-2	10" GT	O	MTH	2	Ground Track
Total:	62					

68. MTH Real Trax O Scale Track 143" x 152"

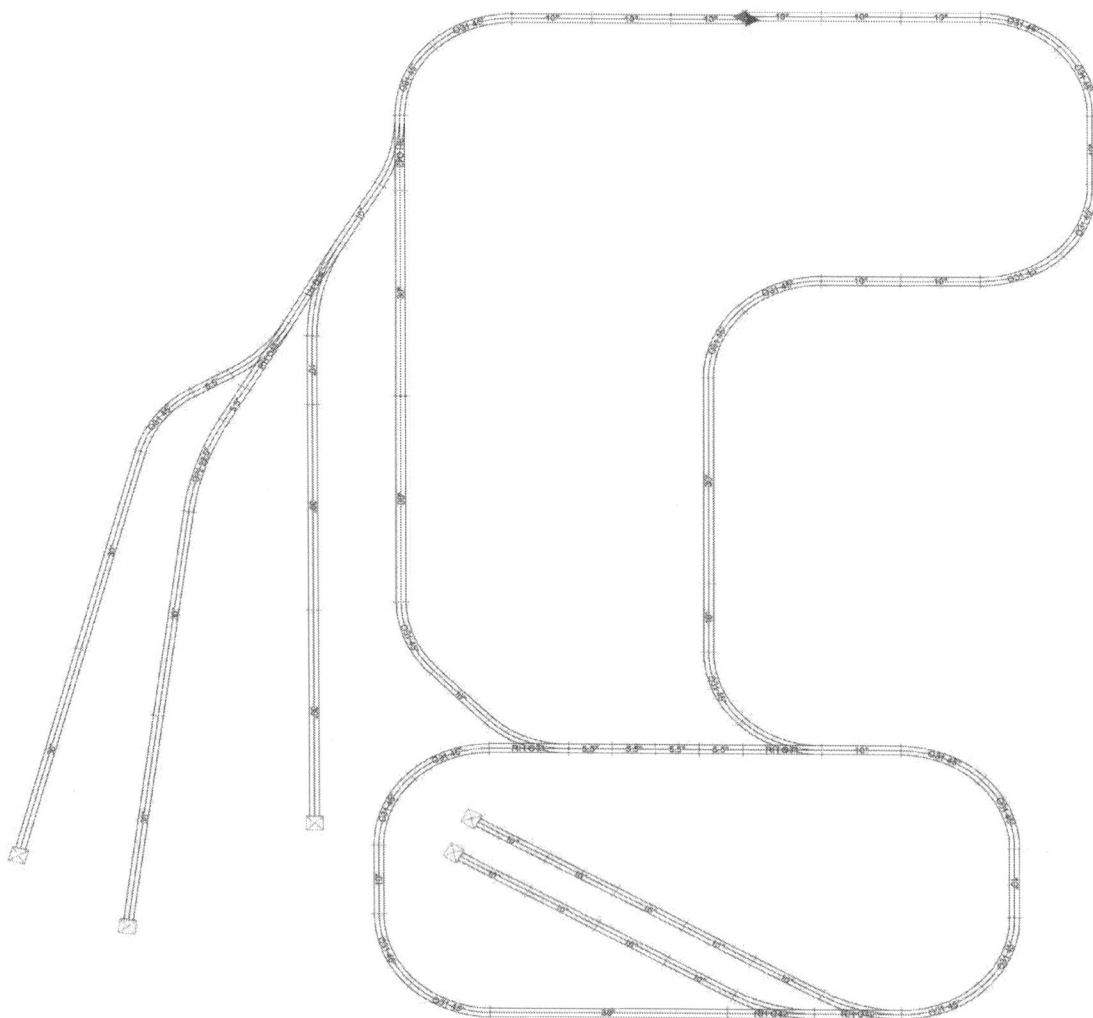

	Part #	Type	Brand	Qty.	
1	40-1001	10" O	MTH	25	
2	40-1002	O31 45° O	MTH	19	
3	40-1004	RH O31 O	MTH	2	
4	40-1010	O72 22.5° O	MTH	1	
5	40-1012	5.5" O	MTH	6	
6	40-1019	30" O	MTH	10	
7	40-1024	Bmp O	MTH	5	Lighted bumper
8	40-1043	RH O42 O	MTH	4	
9	40-1056	LH O54 O	MTH	1	

Total: 73

69. Lionel O Scale Fastrack 136" x 144

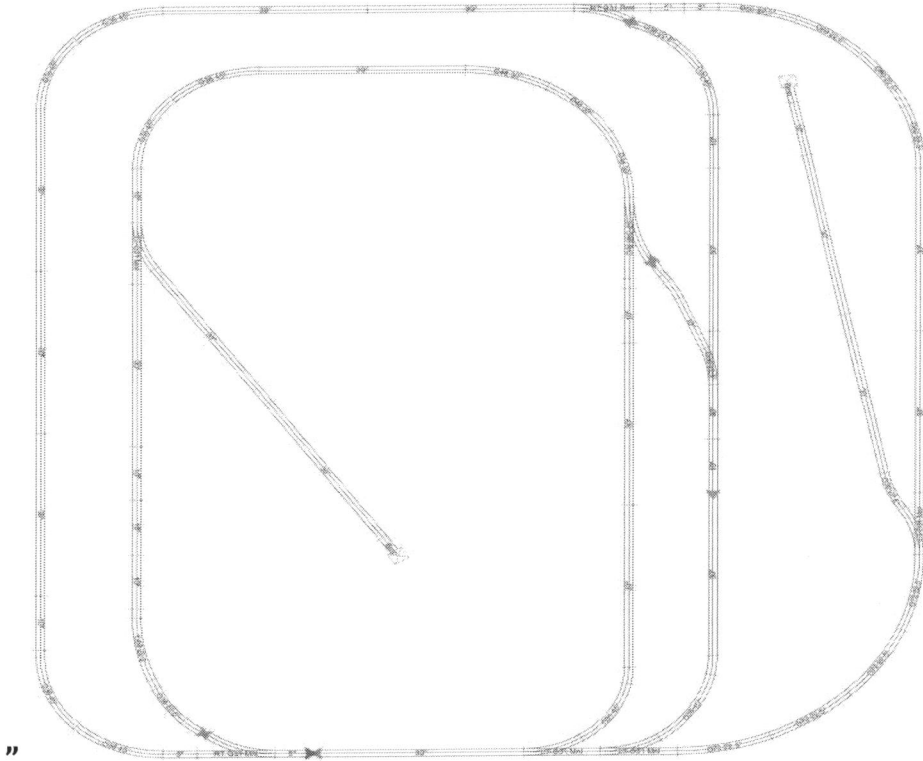

"

	Part #	Type		Brand	Qty.	
1	6-12014	10"	O	Lionel	11	
2	6-12015	O36 45°	O	Lionel	8	
3	6-12022	O36 22.5°	O	Lionel	4	
4	6-12023	O36 11.25°	O	Lionel	3	
5	6-12024	5"	O	Lionel	4	
6	6-12026	1 3/4"	O	Lionel	4	
7	6-12035	Bmp	O	Lionel	2	Bumper, lighted
8	6-12041	O72 22.5°	O	Lionel	4	
9	6-12042	30"	O	Lionel	19	
10	6-12043	O48 30°	O	Lionel	3	
11	6-12056	O60 22.5°	O	Lionel	5	
12	6-12073	1 3/8"	O	Lionel	3	
13	6-37103	O31 45°	O	Lionel	1	
14	6-81251	RT O31 Mnl	O	Lionel	1	
15	6-81252	LT O31 Mnl	O	Lionel	4	
16	6-81253	RT O31 Rmt	O	Lionel	1	
17	6-81662	O31 11.25°	O	Lionel	2	
18	6-81949	LT O48 R/C	O	Lionel	1	

Total: 80

70. Lionel O Scale Fastrack 313" x 76"

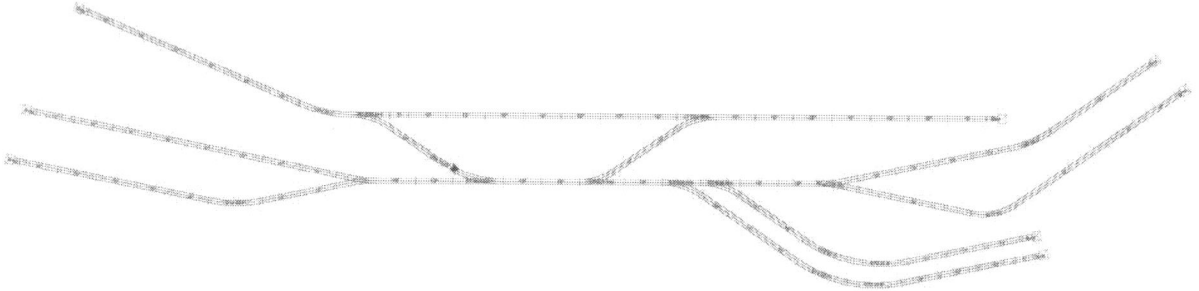

	Part #	Type	Brand	Qty.	
1	6-12014	10" O	Lionel	62	
2	6-12018	RT O36 Mnl O	Lionel	3	
3	6-12024	5" O	Lionel	2	
4	6-12026	1 3/4" O	Lionel	1	
5	6-12035	Bmp O	Lionel	2	Bumper, lighted
6	6-12041	O72 22.5° O	Lionel	6	
7	6-12042	30" O	Lionel	3	
8	6-12045	LT O36 Rmt O	Lionel	1	
9	6-12047	Wye O72 Rmt O	Lionel	1	
10	6-12056	O60 22.5° O	Lionel	1	
11	6-12059	Bmp O	Lionel	6	Bumper, wood
12	6-12061	O84 11.25° O	Lionel	1	
13	6-16829	RT O60 CC O	Lionel	1	
14	6-16832	Wye O72 CC O	Lionel	1	
15	6-37103	O31 45° O	Lionel	1	
16	6-81252	LT O31 Mnl O	Lionel	1	

Total: 93

71. Lionel O27 O Scale Track 204" x 133"

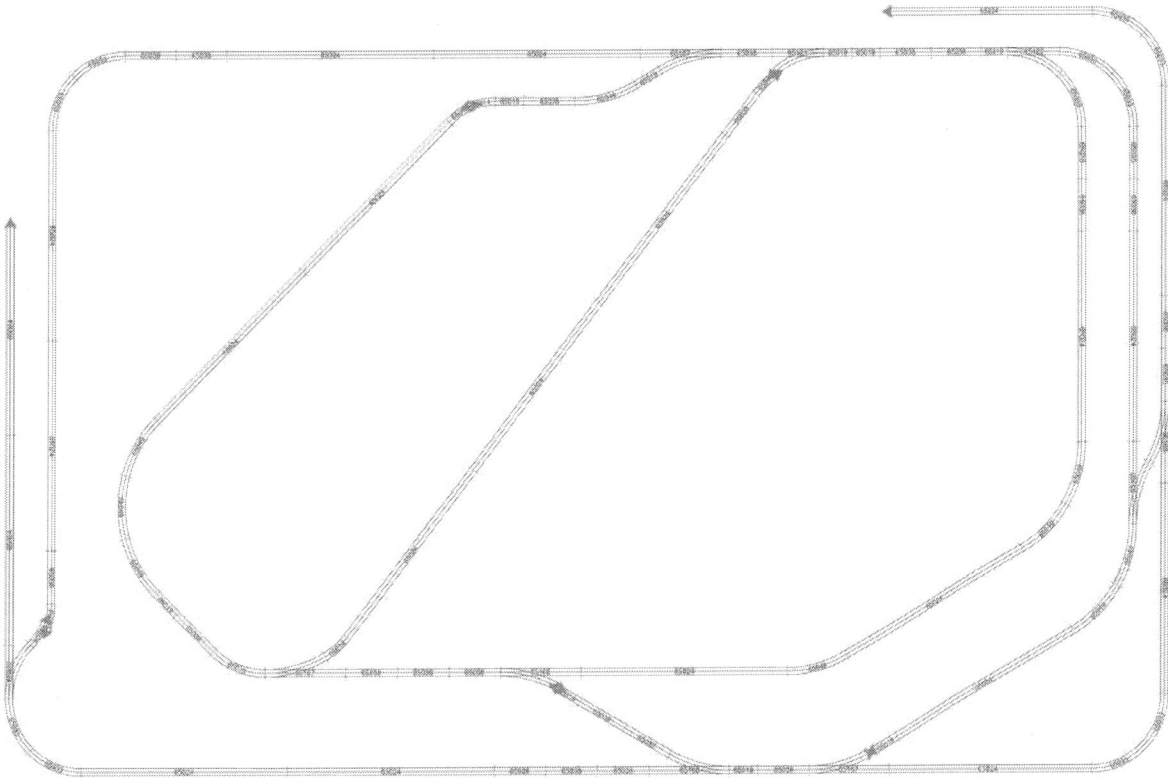

	Part #	Type		Brand	Qty.
1	6-65014	65014	O27	Lionel	6
2	6-65019	65019	O27	Lionel	9
3	6-65022	65022	O27	Lionel	1
4	6-65024	65024	O27	Lionel	22
5	6-65033	65033	O27	Lionel	12
6	6-65038	65038	O27	Lionel	24
7	6-65049	65049	O27	Lionel	9
8	6-65121	65121	O27	Lionel	1
9	6-65122	65122	O27	Lionel	1
10	6-65167	65167	O27	Lionel	3
11	6-65168	65168	O27	Lionel	4

Total: 92

72. Lionel O27 O Scale Track 204" x 147"

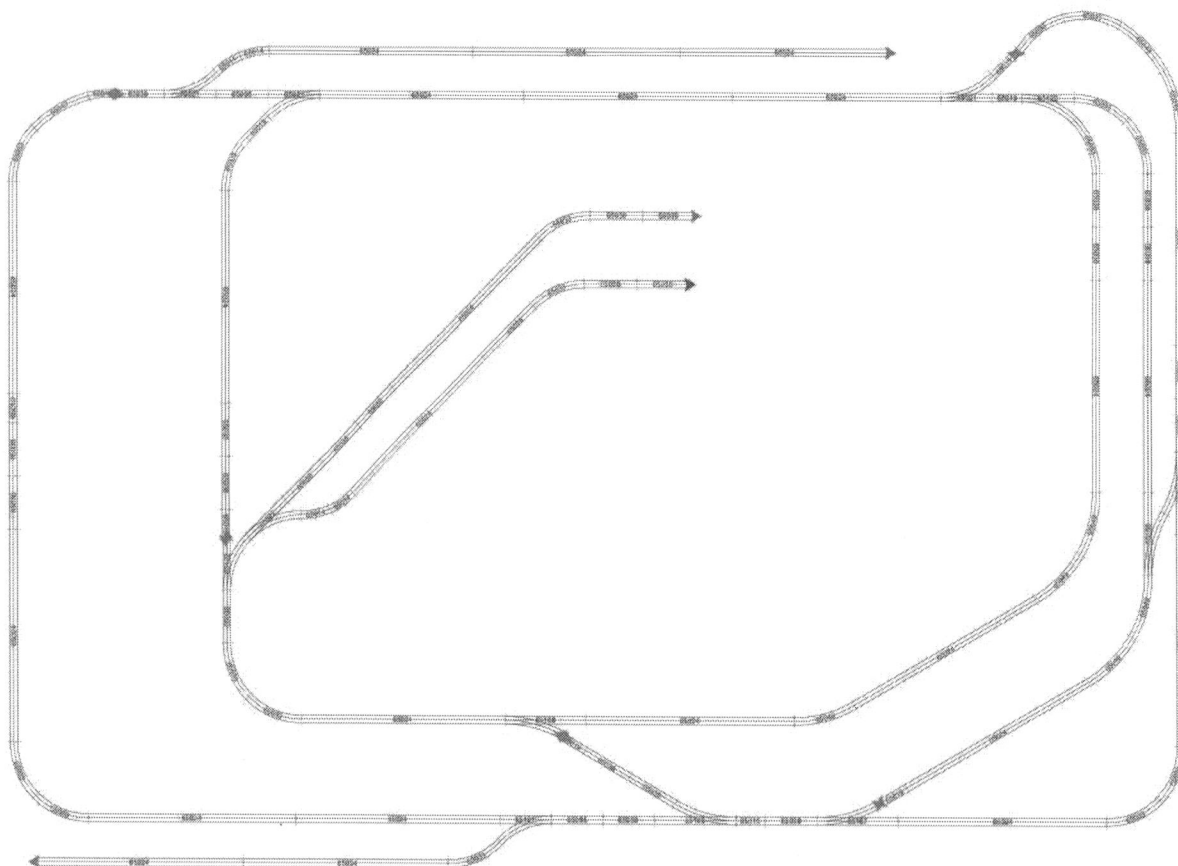

	Part #	Type	Brand	Qty.
1	6-65014	65014	O27	Lionel	5
2	6-65019	65019	O27	Lionel	8
3	6-65021	65021	O27	Lionel	3
4	6-65022	65022	O27	Lionel	1
5	6-65024	65024	O27	Lionel	24
6	6-65033	65033	O27	Lionel	16
7	6-65038	65038	O27	Lionel	26
8	6-65049	65049	O27	Lionel	8
9	6-65121	65121	O27	Lionel	1
10	6-65122	65122	O27	Lionel	2
11	6-65167	65167	O27	Lionel	1
12	6-65168	65168	O27	Lionel	4

Total: 99

73. Lionel O27 O Scale Track 215" x 129"

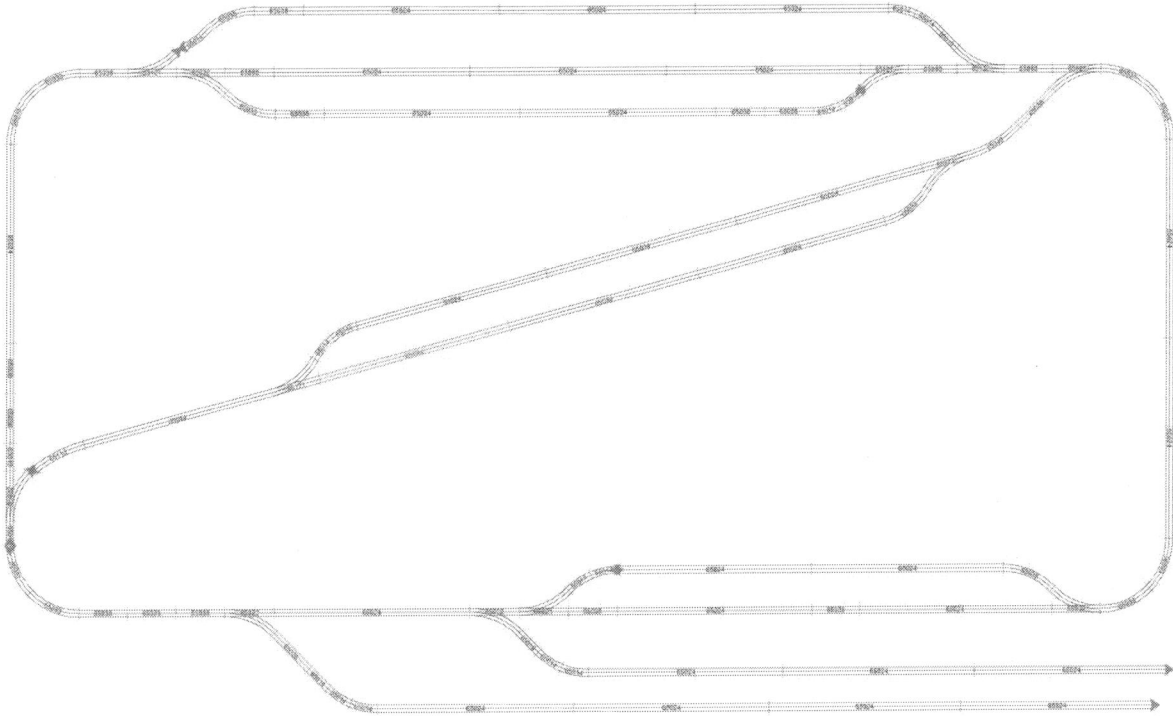

	Part #	Type		Brand	Qty.
1	6-65014	65014	O27	Lionel	13
2	6-65019	65019	O27	Lionel	5
3	6-65021	65021	O27	Lionel	2
4	6-65022	65022	O27	Lionel	5
5	6-65024	65024	O27	Lionel	30
6	6-65033	65033	O27	Lionel	12
7	6-65038	65038	O27	Lionel	17
8	6-65049	65049	O27	Lionel	1
9	6-65113	65113	O27	Lionel	1
10	6-65121	65121	O27	Lionel	4
11	6-65122	65122	O27	Lionel	1

Total: 91

74. Lionel O27 O Scale Track 224" x 112"

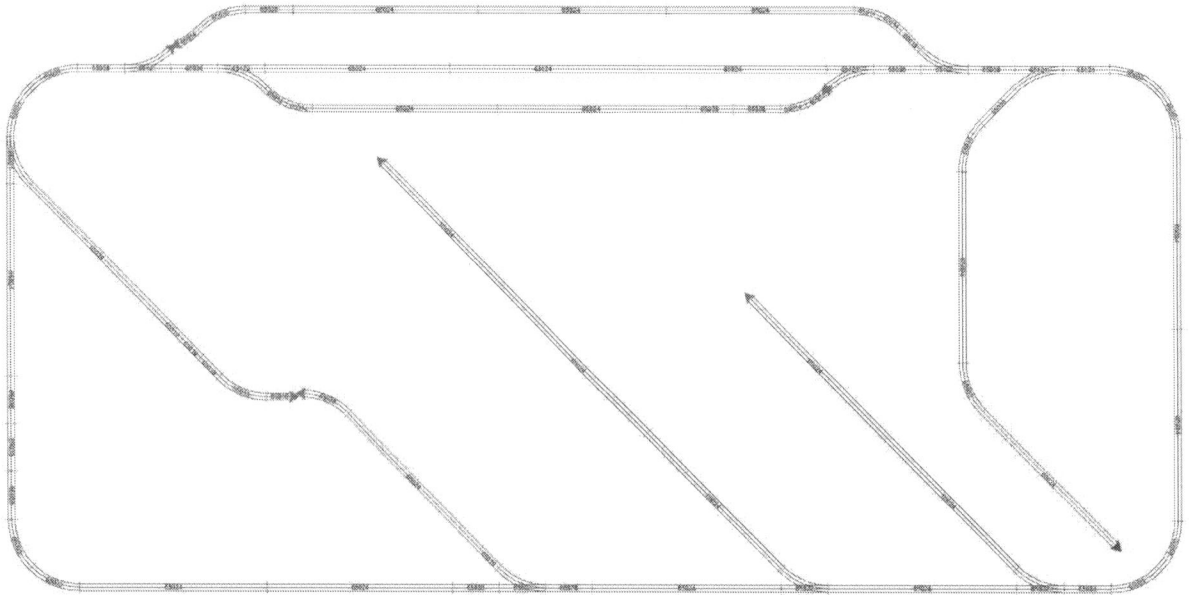

	Part #	Type	Brand	Qty.
1	6-65014	65014 O27	Lionel	7
2	6-65019	65019 O27	Lionel	6
3	6-65021	65021 O27	Lionel	1
4	6-65022	65022 O27	Lionel	3
5	6-65024	65024 O27	Lionel	24
6	6-65033	65033 O27	Lionel	13
7	6-65038	65038 O27	Lionel	15
8	6-65121	65121 O27	Lionel	3
9	6-65122	65122 O27	Lionel	2

Total: 74

75. Atlas O Scale 3-Rail Track 173" x 187"

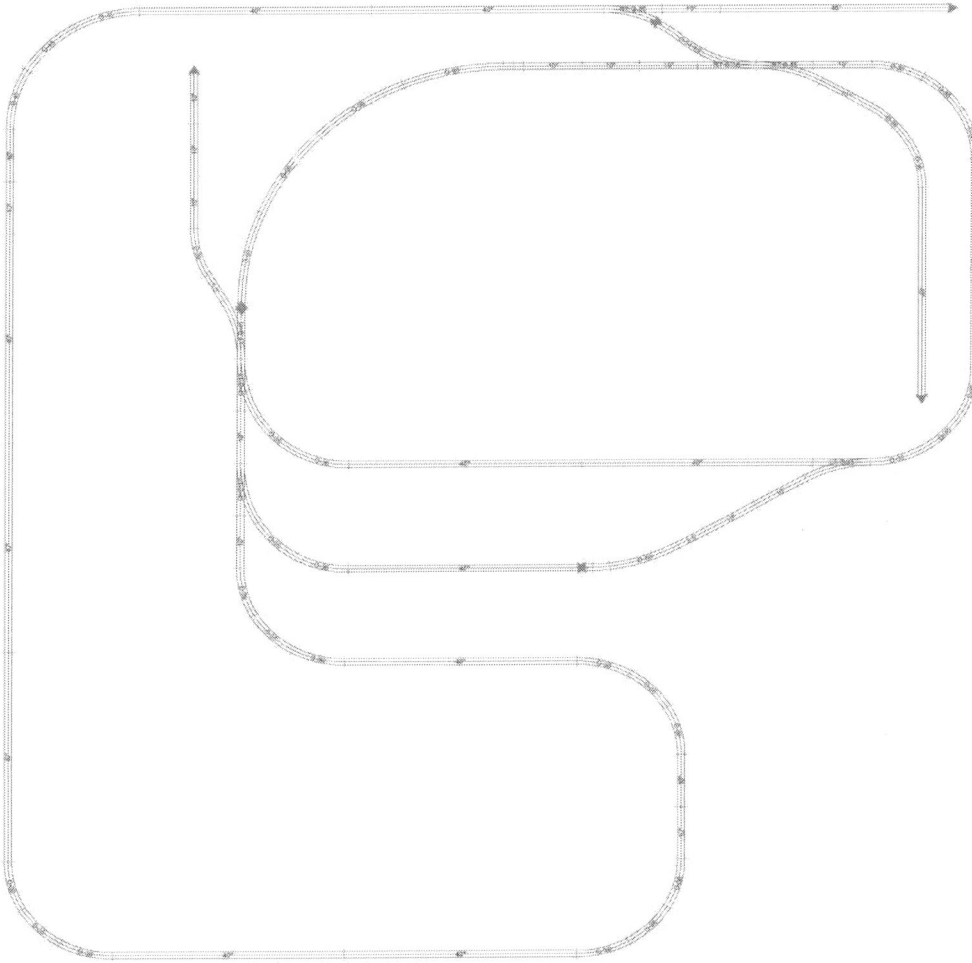

	Part #		Type	Brand	Qty.
1	6013	O-90	O	Atlas	4
2	6015	1.25"	O	Atlas	1
3	6045	O-45	O	Atlas	3
4	6046	O-45 1/4	O	Atlas	1
5	6050	10"	O	Atlas	17
6	6052	1.75"	O	Atlas	3
7	6053	5.5"	O	Atlas	2
8	6058	40"	O	Atlas	14
9	6061	O-54 1/2	O	Atlas	1
10	6064	O-63	O	Atlas	1
11	6066	O-36	O	Atlas	25
12	6068	O-36 1/4	O	Atlas	2
13	6076	RT O-36	O	Atlas	2
14	6085	LT O-45	O	Atlas	4
15	6086	RT O-45	O	Atlas	1

Total: 81

76. Atlas O Scale 3-Rail 163" x 187"

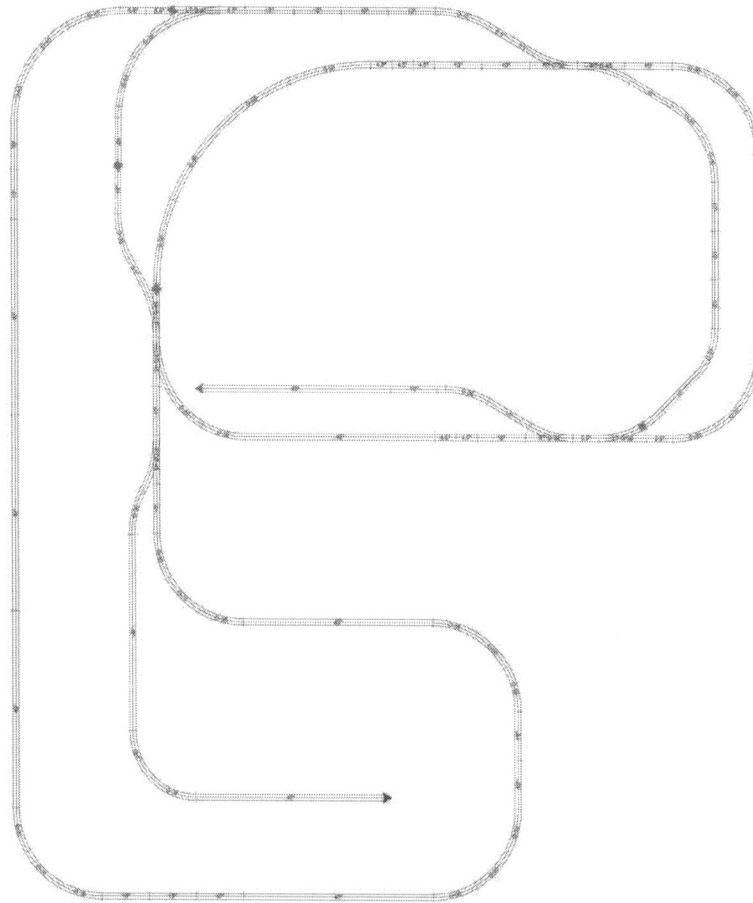

	Part #	Type		Brand	Qty.
1	6013	O-90	O	Atlas	4
2	6015	1.25"	O	Atlas	1
3	6043	O-27	O	Atlas	3
4	6045	O-45	O	Atlas	4
5	6046	O-45 1/4	O	Atlas	1
6	6050	10"	O	Atlas	26
7	6051	4.5"	O	Atlas	5
8	6052	1.75"	O	Atlas	1
9	6053	5.5"	O	Atlas	8
10	6058	40"	O	Atlas	10
11	6060	O-54	O	Atlas	1
12	6066	O-36	O	Atlas	26
13	6068	O-36 1/4	O	Atlas	2
14	6075	LT O-36	O	Atlas	1
15	6076	RT O-36	O	Atlas	2
16	6085	LT O-45	O	Atlas	3
17	6086	RT O-45	O	Atlas	2
Total:	100				

77. MTH O Scale Scale-Tracks 210" x 107"

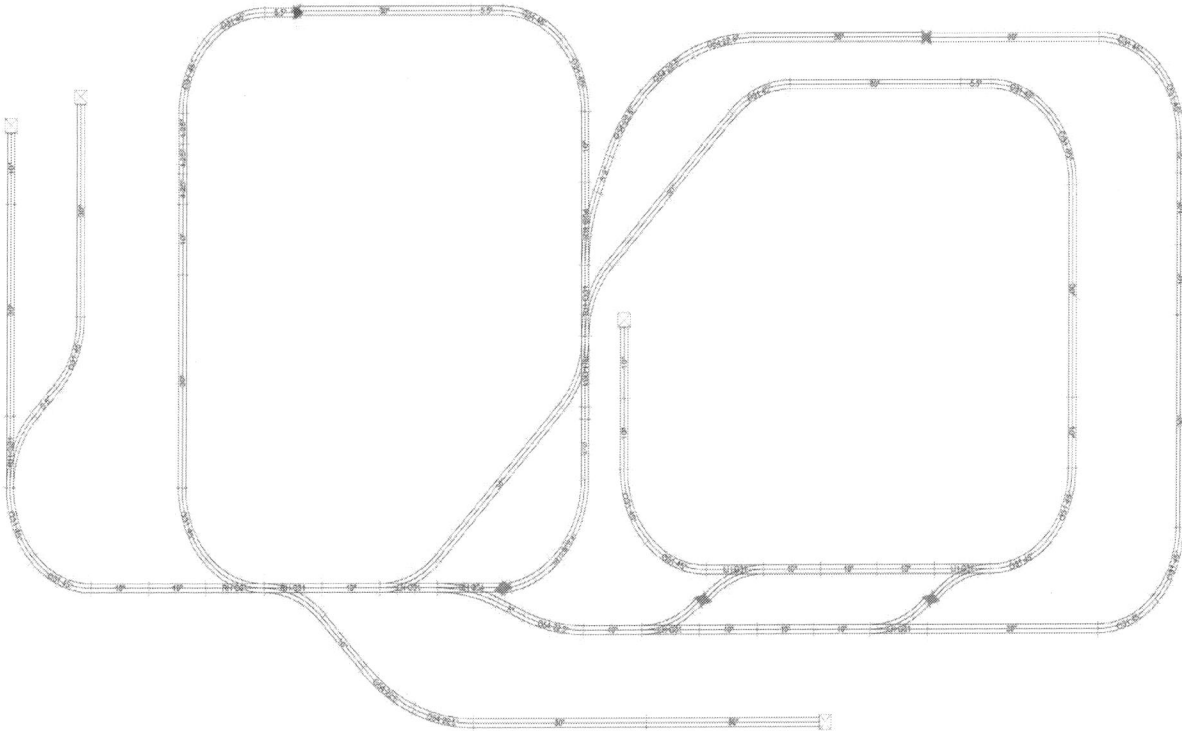

	Part #	Type		Brand	Qty.	
1	45-1001	10"	O	MTH	19	
2	45-1002	O31 45°	O	MTH	19	
3	45-1003	LH O31	O	MTH	5	
4	45-1004	RH O31	O	MTH	5	
5	45-1007	O54 22.5°	O	MTH	6	
6	45-1009	RH O54	O	MTH	2	
7	45-1011	1.75"	O	MTH	2	
8	45-1012	4.25"	O	MTH	3	
9	45-1013	5"	O	MTH	2	
10	45-1014	5.5"	O	MTH	5	
11	45-1019	30"	O	MTH	14	
12	45-1025	Bmp	O	MTH	4	Track end
13	45-1049	30"/Flex	O	MTH	1	

Total: 87

78. MTH O Scale Scale Tracks 199" x 225"

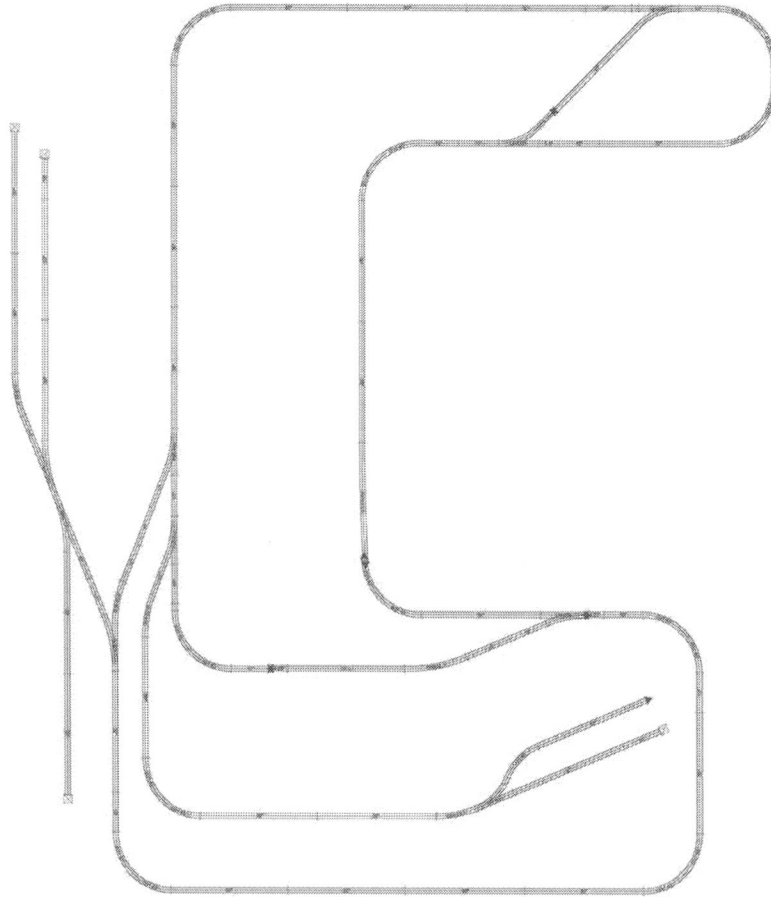

	Part #	Type	Brand	Qty.	
1	45-1001	10" O	MTH	22	
2	45-1002	O31 45°	O	MTH	21
3	45-1003	LH O31 O	MTH	3	
4	45-1007	O54 22.5°	O	MTH	4
5	45-1008	LH O54 O	MTH	1	
6	45-1009	RH O54 O	MTH	2	
7	45-1011	1.75" O	MTH	4	
8	45-1012	4.25" O	MTH	2	
9	45-1013	5" O	MTH	1	
10	45-1014	5.5" O	MTH	2	
11	45-1019	30" O	MTH	28	
12	45-1020	RH O72 O	MTH	2	
13	45-1021	LH O72 O	MTH	1	
14	45-1025	Bmp O	MTH	4	Track end
15	45-1034	O80 22.5°	O	MTH	1
16	45-1049	30"/Flex	O	MTH	2

Total: 100

79.   G SCALE ARISTOCRAT G TRACK 254" X 265"

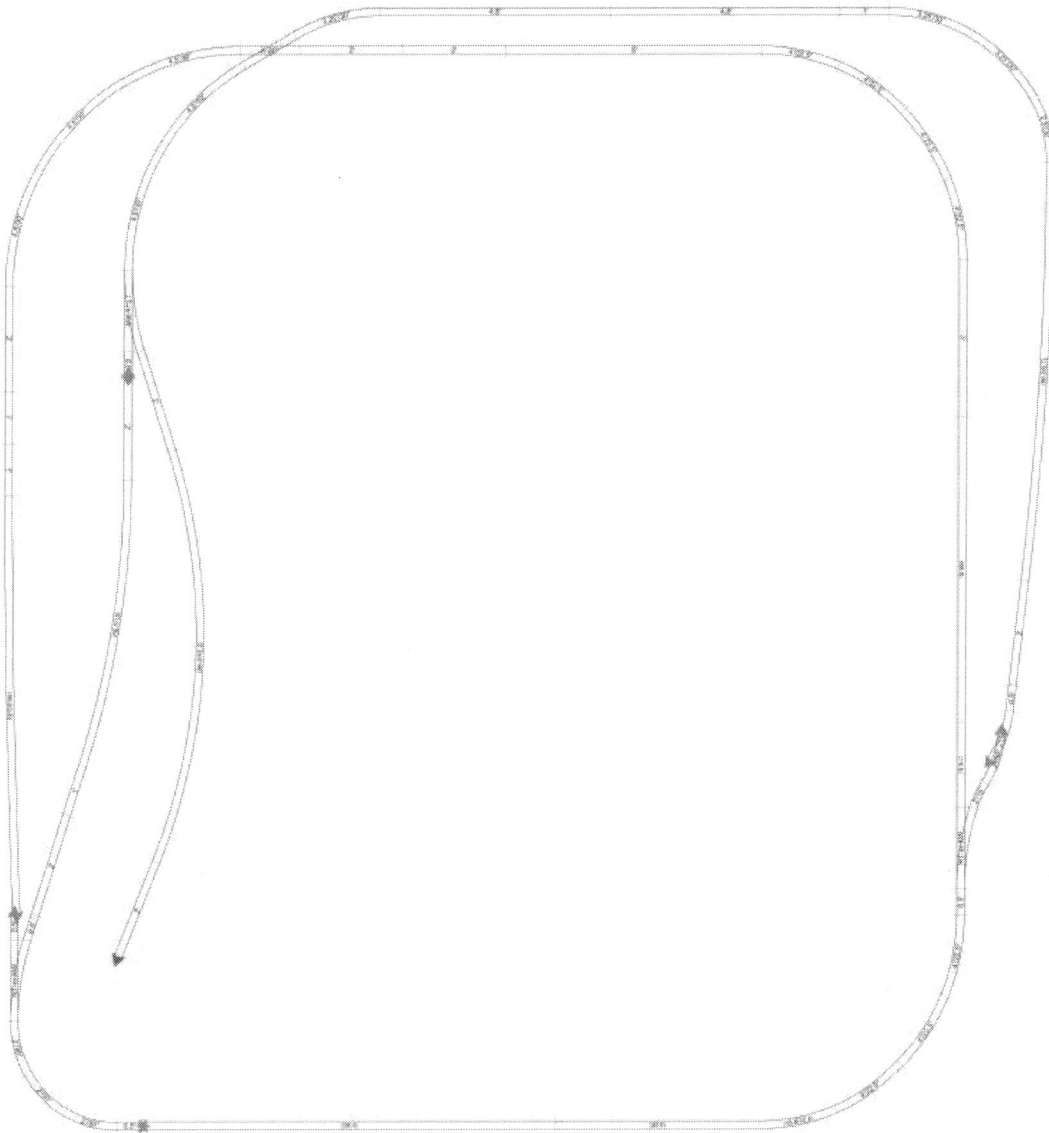

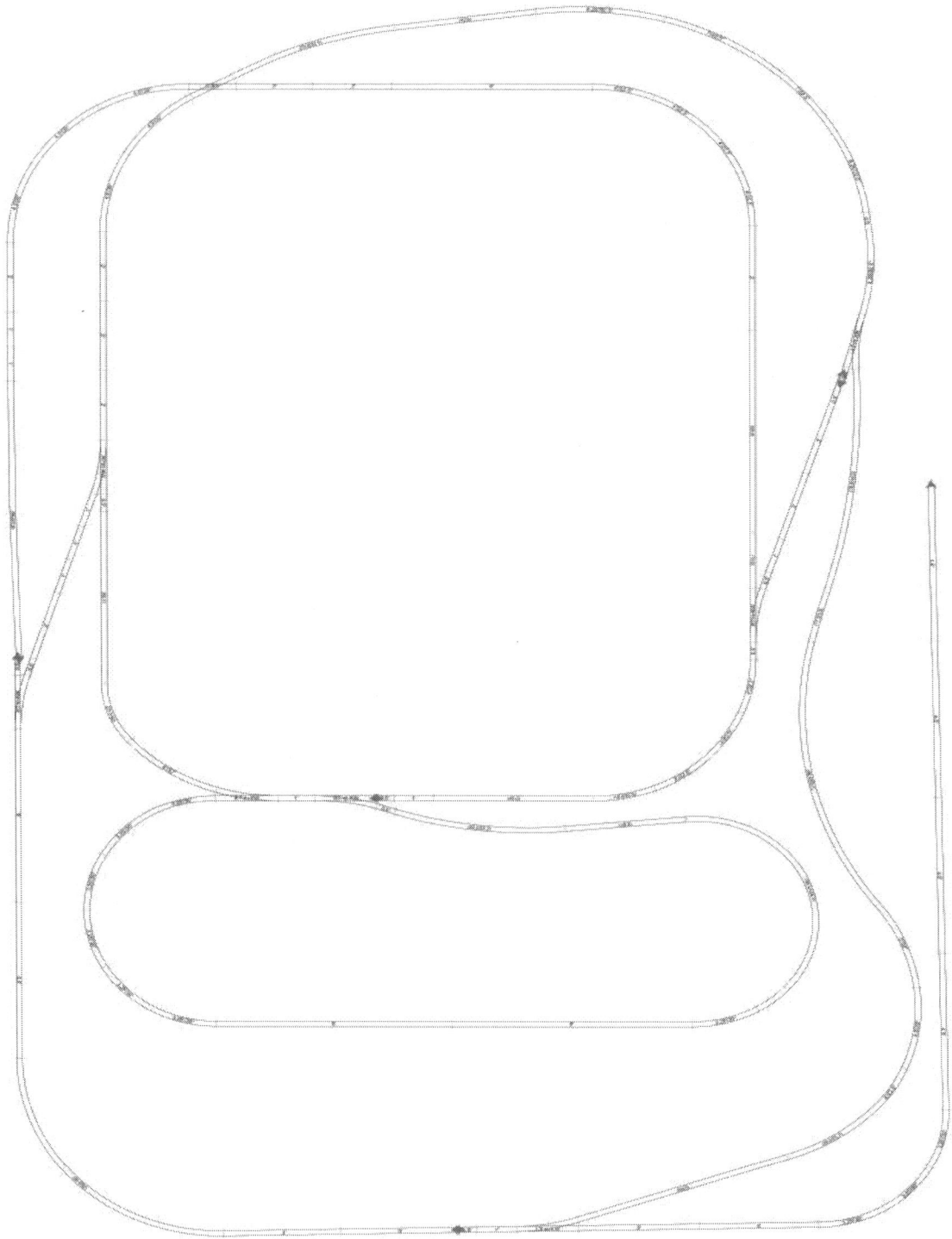

81. G SCALE BACHMANN G TRACK 164" X 105"

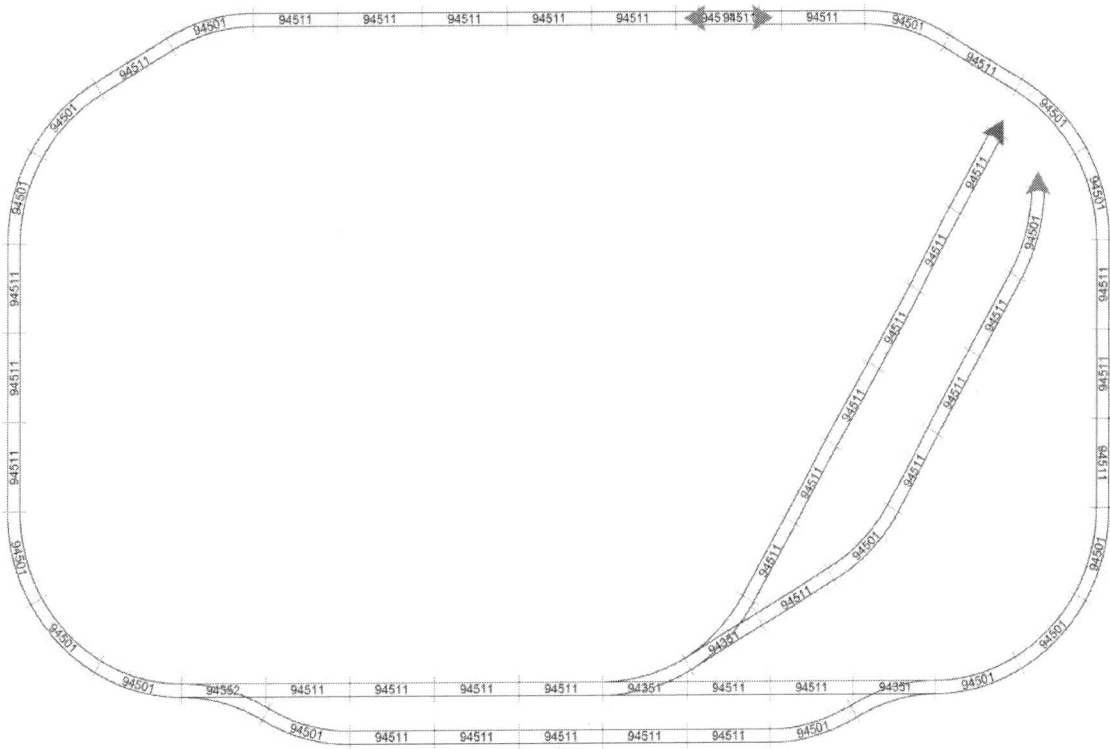

82. G SCALE LGB G TRACK 235" X 226"

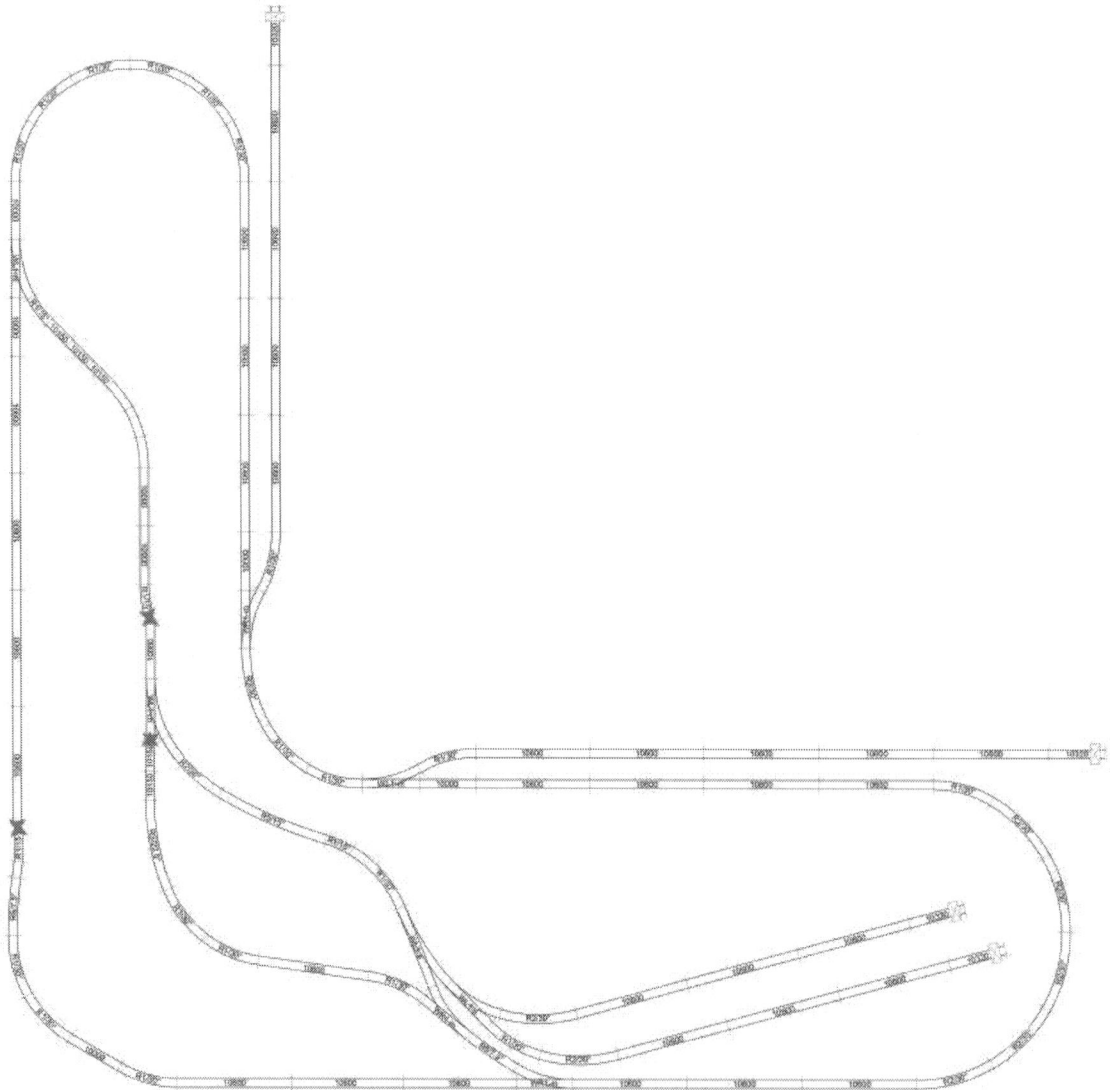

83.   G SCALE LGB G TRACK 286" X 93"

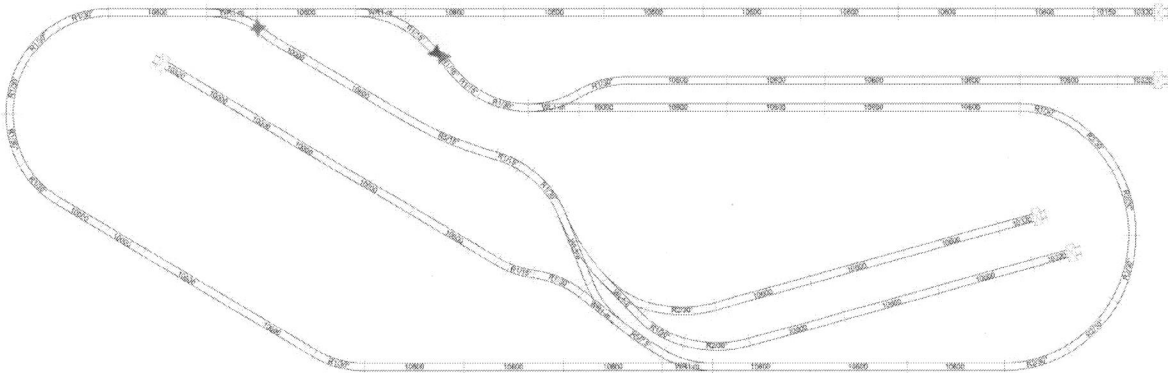

84.   G SCALE LGB G TRACK 286" X 176"

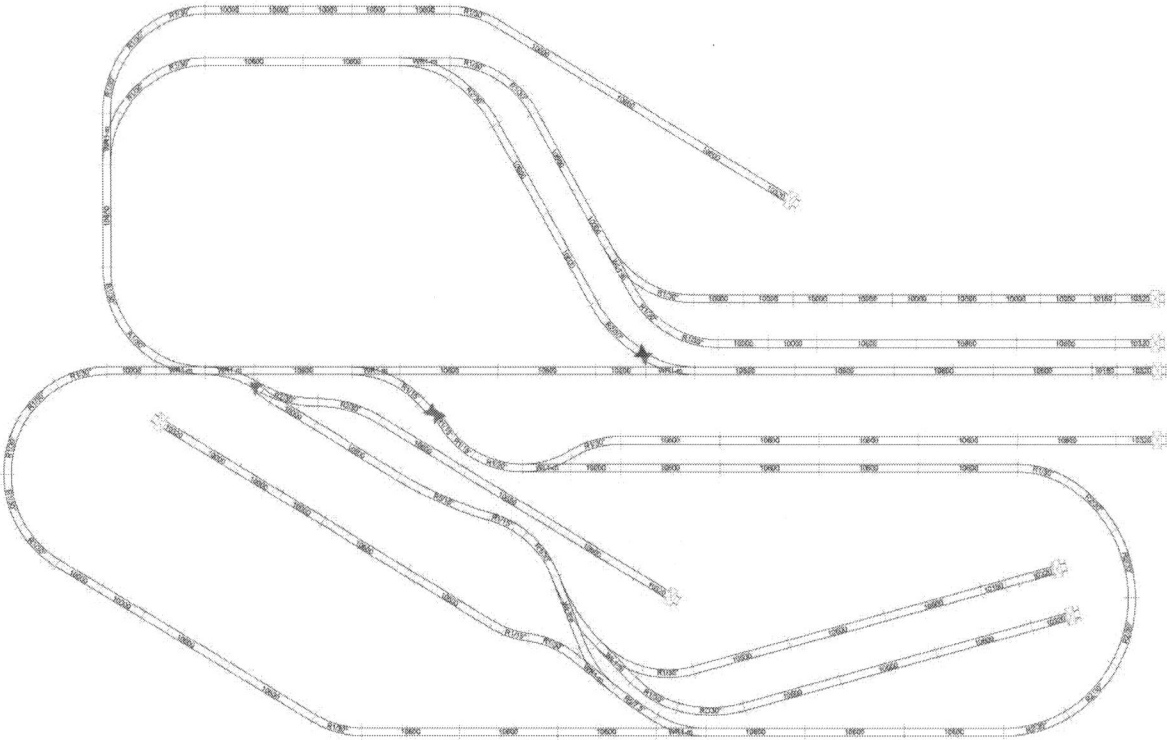

85. Aristocrat G Scale G USA Track 348" x 314"

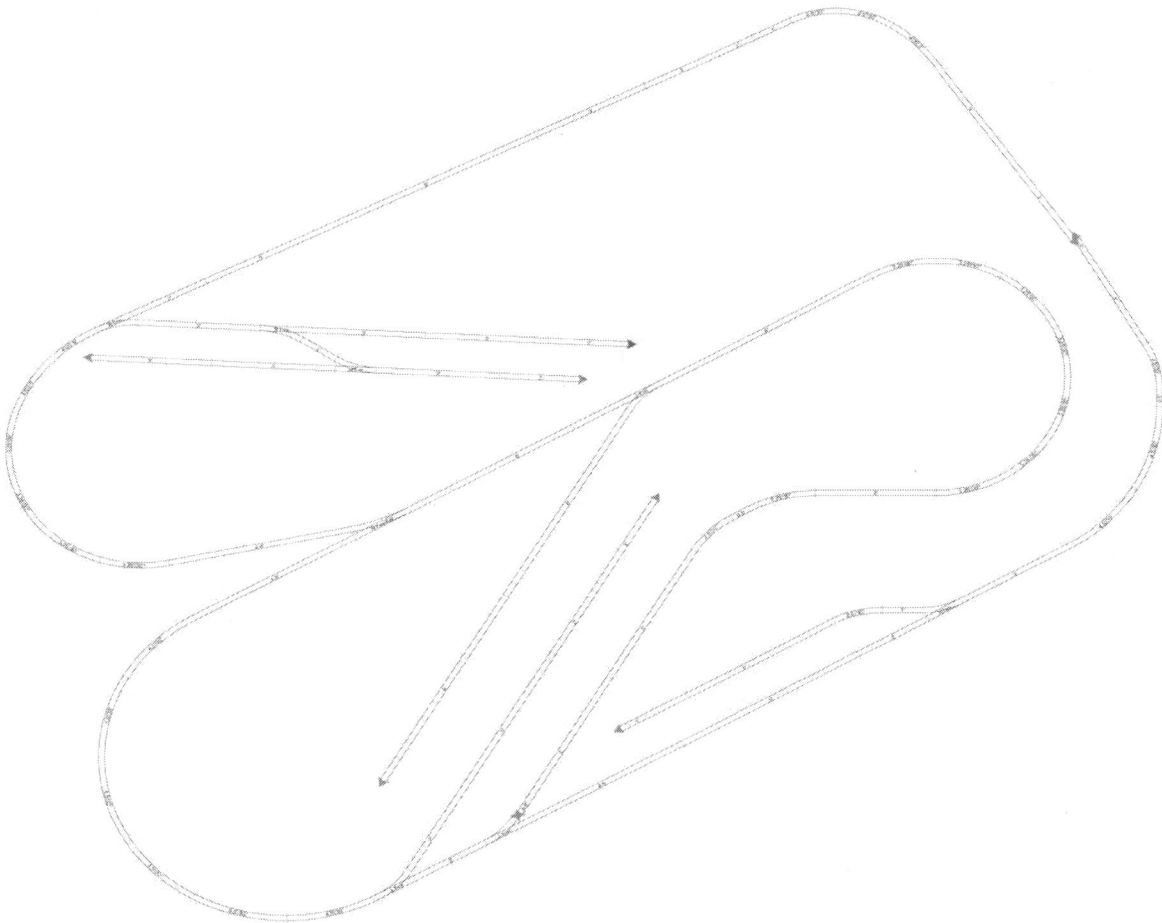

	Part #		Type	Brand	Qty.	
1	30030	1'	G	Aristo-Craft	5	
2	30031	0.5'	G	Aristo-Craft	4	
3	30060	2'	G	Aristo-Craft	8	
4	30090	3'	G	Aristo-Craft	15	
5	30110	2.5'/30°	G	Aristo-Craft	5	
6	30112	3.25'/30°	G	Aristo-Craft	12	
7	30115	4'/22.5°	G	Aristo-Craft	3	
8	30116	4.5'/30°	G	Aristo-Craft	8	
9	30193	4.5'	G	Aristo-Craft	3	
10	30195	5'	G	Aristo-Craft	4	
11	30196	6'	G	Aristo-Craft	2	
12	30197	6'	G	Aristo-Craft	3	
13	30300	RT-m	G	Aristo-Craft	4	Manual operated turnout
14	30350	LT-m	G	Aristo-Craft	3	Manual operated turnout
15	30370	RT-m XW	G	Aristo-Craft	1	Manual operated turnout

Total: 80

86. Aristocrat G Scale G USA Track 363" x 238"

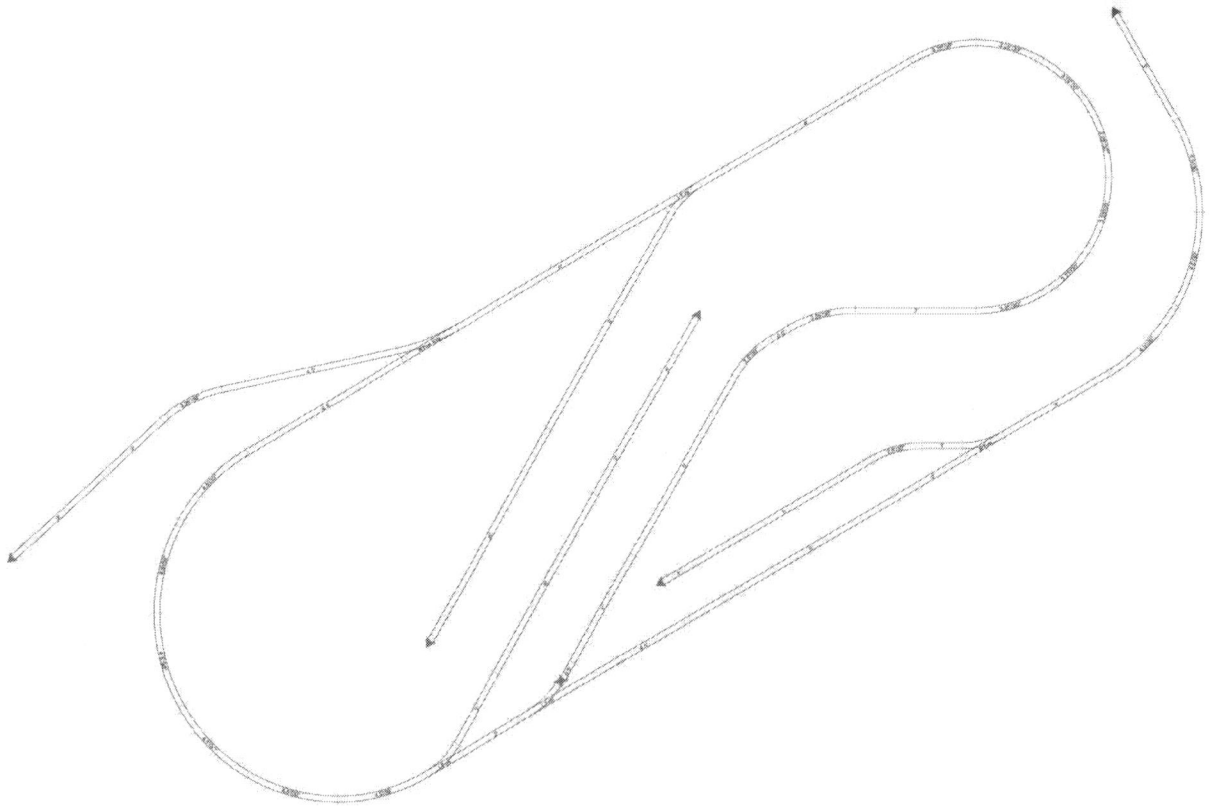

	Part #		Type	Brand	Qty.	
1	30030	1'	G	Aristo-Craft	2	
2	30031	0.5'	G	Aristo-Craft	2	
3	30060	2'	G	Aristo-Craft	5	
4	30090	3'	G	Aristo-Craft	6	
5	30110	2.5'/30°	G	Aristo-Craft	2	
6	30112	3.25'/30°	G	Aristo-Craft	9	
7	30116	4.5'/30°	G	Aristo-Craft	9	
8	30193	4.5'	G	Aristo-Craft	3	
9	30195	5'	G	Aristo-Craft	4	
10	30196	6'	G	Aristo-Craft	1	
11	30197	6'	G	Aristo-Craft	3	
12	30300	RT-m	G	Aristo-Craft	1	Manual operated turnout
13	30350	LT-m	G	Aristo-Craft	3	Manual operated turnout
14	30370	RT-m XW	G	Aristo-Craft	1	Manual operated turnout

Total: 51

87. LGB G Scale Track 277" x 219"

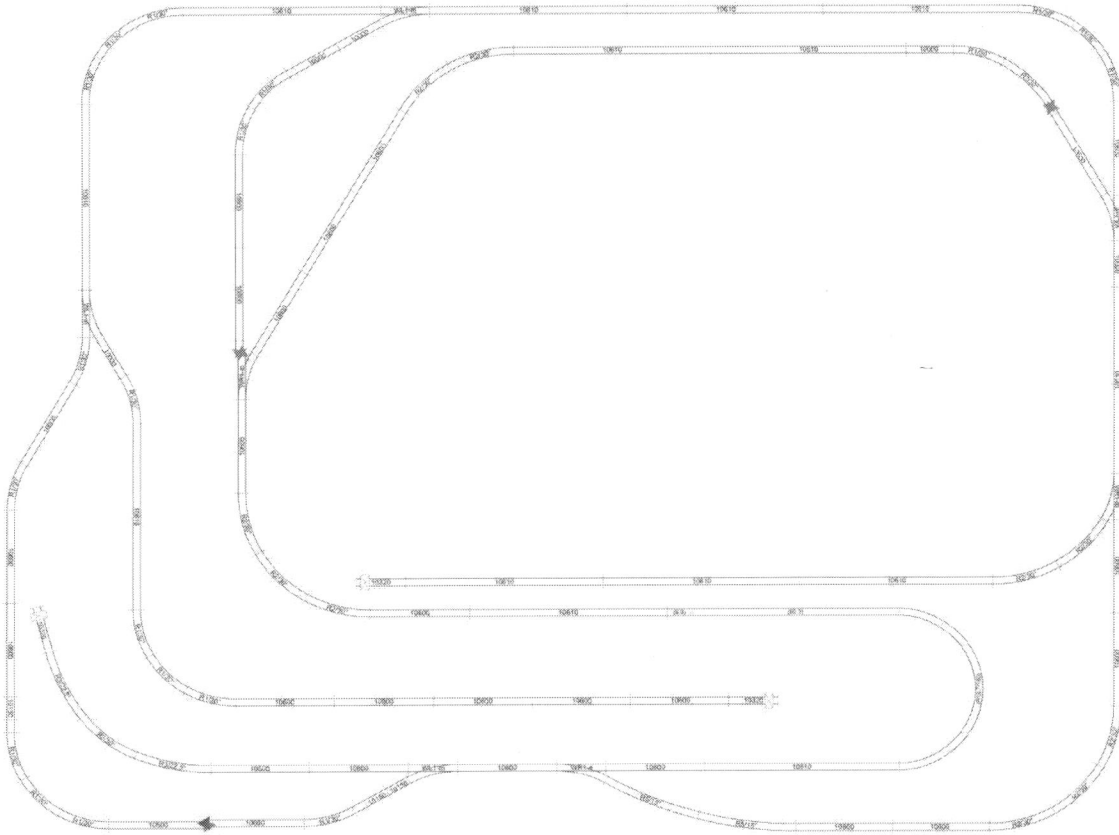

	Part #		Type	Brand	Qty.				
1	10000	10000 G		LGB	5				
2	10006x2+10003x10		Flex/Long		G		LGB	1	
3	10040	10040 G		LGB	1				
4	10050	10050 G		LGB	1				
5	10070	10070 G		LGB	1				
6	10080	10080 G		LGB	2				
7	10150	10150 G		LGB	3				
8	10320	10320 G		LGB	3		Buffer, old style		
9	10600	10600 G		LGB	27				
10	10610	10610 G		LGB	14				
11	11000	R1/30° G		LGB	19				
12	12000	WR1-m G		LGB	2				
13	12050	WR1-e G		LGB	1				
14	12100	WL1-m G		LGB	4				
15	15000	R2/30° G		LGB	12				
16	16000	R3/22.5°		G	LGB	2			
17	18000	R5/15° G		LGB	2				

Total: 100

88. LGB G Scale Track 337" x 317"

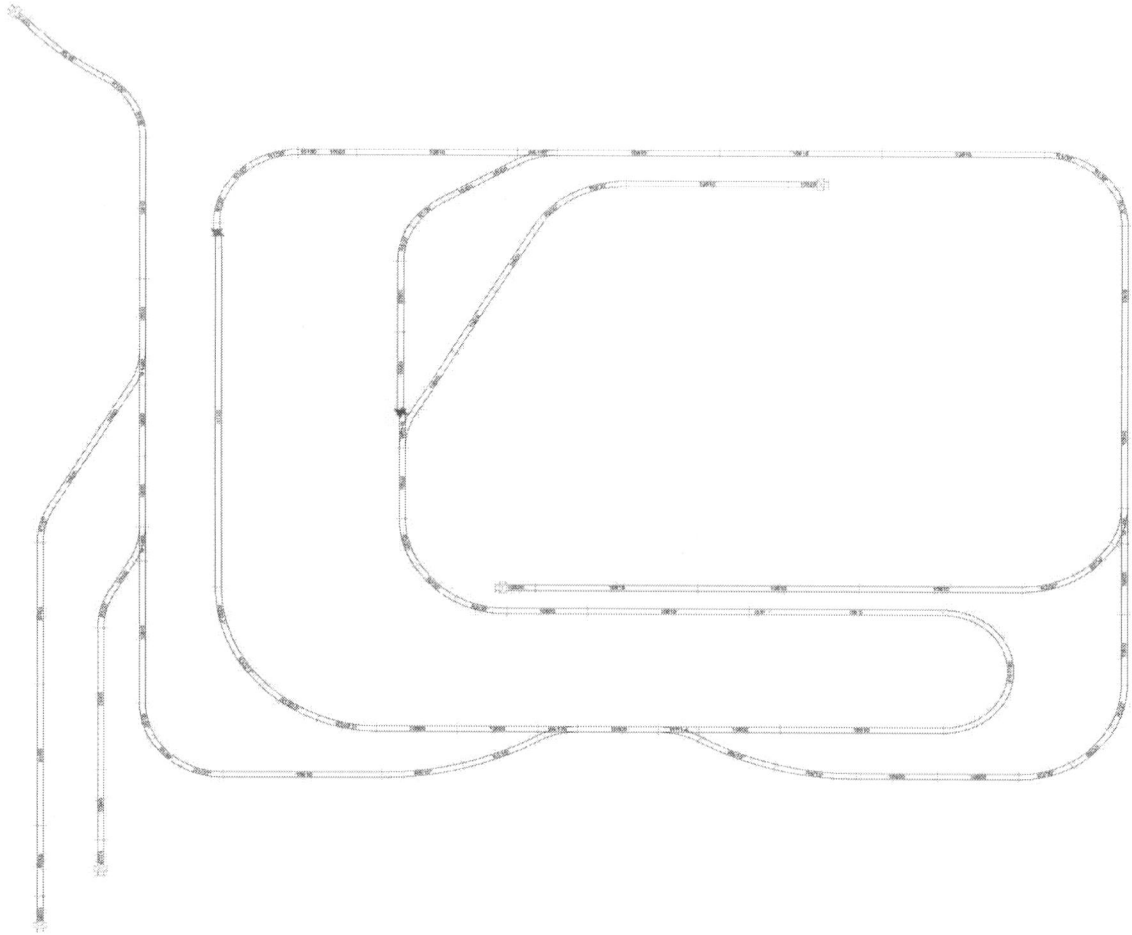

Part #   Type   Brand Qty.

	Part #	Type	Brand	Qty.	
1	10000	10000 G	LGB	4	
2	10006x2+10003x10	Flex/Long	G	LGB	2
3	10050	10050 G	LGB	1	
4	10070	10070 G	LGB	2	
5	10150	10150 G	LGB	1	
6	10320	10320 G	LGB	5	Buffer, old style
7	10600	10600 G	LGB	22	
8	10610	10610 G	LGB	18	
9	11000	R1/30° G	LGB	15	
10	12000	WR1-m G	LGB	4	
11	12050	WR1-e G	LGB	1	
12	12100	WL1-m G	LGB	2	
13	15000	R2/30° G	LGB	10	
14	16000	R3/22.5°	G	LGB	4
15	18000	R5/15° G	LGB	5	
Total:	96				

89. LGB G Scale Track 516" x 288"

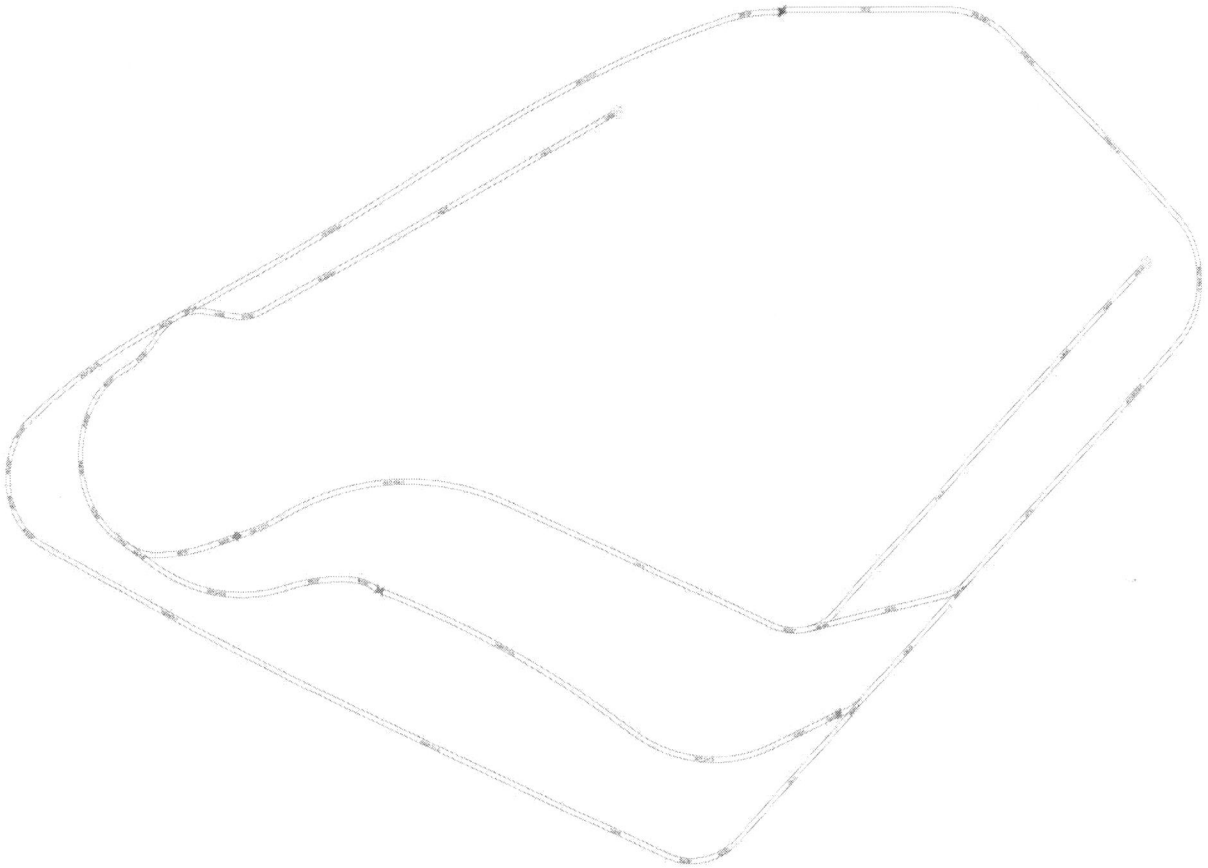

Part #   Type   Brand Qty.

#	Part #		Type		Brand	Qty.	
1	10000	10000 G	LGB	2			
2	10005x2+10003x5		Flex/Short	G	LGB	5	
3	10006x2+10003x10		Flex/Long	G	LGB	11	
4	10070	10070 G	LGB	2			
5	10150	10150 G	LGB	2			
6	10320	10320 G	LGB	2		Buffer, old style	
7	10600	10600 G	LGB	3			
8	10610	10610 G	LGB	5			
9	11000	R1/30° G	LGB	6			
10	11040	R1/7.5°G	LGB	1			
11	12000	WR1-m G	LGB	2			
12	12050	WR1-e G	LGB	1			
13	12100	WL1-m G	LGB	3			
14	15000	R2/30° G	LGB	8			
15	18000	R5/15° G	LGB	3			

Total: 56

90. LGB G Scale Track 592" x 308"

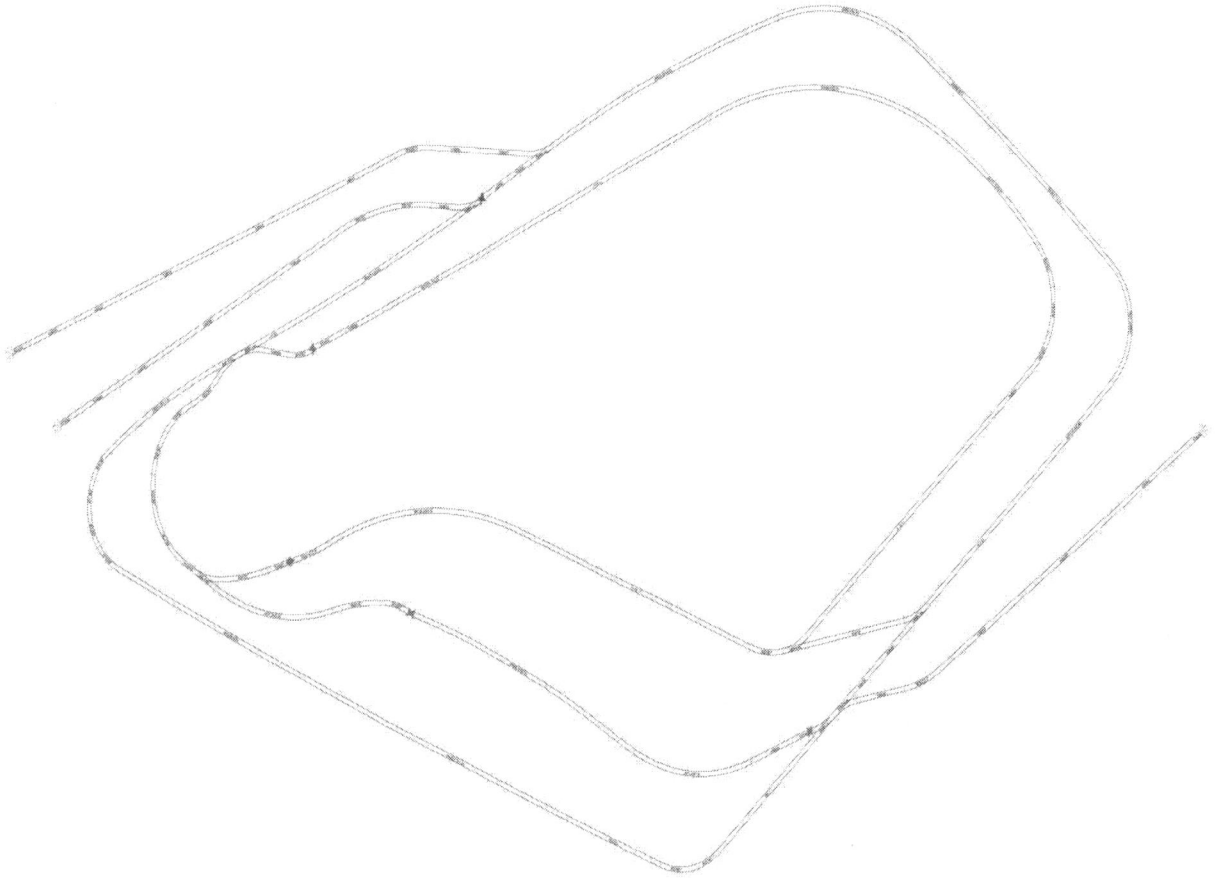

Part #   Type   Brand Qty.

	Part #	Type		Brand	Qty.	
1	10000 10000 G	LGB	6			
2	10005x2+10003x5	Flex/Short	G	LGB	6	
3	10006x2+10003x10	Flex/Long	G	LGB	13	
4	10070 10070 G	LGB	1			
5	10080 10080 G	LGB	2			
6	10150 10150 G	LGB	3			
7	10320 10320 G	LGB	3	Buffer, old style		
8	10600 10600 G	LGB	11			
9	10610 10610 G	LGB	10			
10	11000 R1/30° G	LGB	6			
11	11040 R1/7.5°G	LGB	1			
12	12000 WR1-m G	LGB	5			
13	12050 WR1-e G	LGB	1			
14	12100 WL1-m G	LGB	3			
15	15000 R2/30° G	LGB	11			
16	16000 R3/22.5°	G	LGB	2		
17	18000 R5/15° G	LGB	4			

Total: 88

Additional Resources:

Walthers Yardmaster Club

Membership benefits include a free reference book, free or reduced shipping on orders and 10% off from these manufacturers: Rapido, Busch, Walthers Proto, Atlas, Bachmann, Kato, Peco, Bowser, Faller, Broadway Limited, Walthers Mainline, Walthers Trainline, Walthers Cornerstone, LGB, Noch, Fox Valley, Woodland Scenics, Vollmer, Con-Cor, Viessmann, Kibri and Intermountain.

https://www.walthers.com/yardmasters-club

Worlds Greatest Hobby

Link to the complete Worlds Greatest Hobby Model Trains full tips for building your layout booklet in pdf.

http://wgh.trains.com/-/media/Files/Worlds%20Greatest%20Hobby/2015/wgh_fullbooklet_2014.pdf

Model Railway Engineer

Great tips and step by step guides for wiring, layout design, building inclines, building scenery and much more.

https://modelrailwayengineer.com

Horny Hobbies Forum

Strong community forum with tons of topics of potential interest and lots of active users to answer question you may have.

https://www.hornby.com/us-en/forum

National Model Railroad

The National Model Railroad Association and there model railroad directory of sites you may find useful.

https://www.nmra.org/directory

Model Train Tips

Great blog where you find tons of helpful tips and advice for building your model railway.

http://www.model-train-tips.com/blog/

Building Your Model Railroad

Website with in depth information on wiring track and accessories for cab control and DCC operation of your layout.

http://www.building-your-model-railroad.com/model-railroad-wiring.html

.

Thanks and Enjoy!

Printed in Great Britain
by Amazon